'Even if we have terrible proof that pride in the ethnic and religious heritage can quickly degrade into the fascistic, our vigilance on that score should not displace our love and trust in the good of the indigenous per se. On the contrary, a trust in the staying-power and travel-worthiness of such good should encourage us to credit the possibility of a world where respect for the validity of every tradition will issue in the creation and maintenance of a salubrious political space.'

Seamus Heaney, Nobel Lecture

Barney Norris

PLAYS ONE

Introduction by Alice Hamilton

Visitors

Eventide

While We're Here

Nightfall

OBERON BOOKS
LONDON

WWW.OBERONBOOKS.COM

This collection first published in 2018 by Oberon Books Ltd
521 Caledonian Road, London N7 9RH
Tel: +44 (0) 20 7607 3637 / Fax: +44 (0) 20 7607 3629
e-mail: info@oberonbooks.com
www.oberonbooks.com

PB ISBN: 9781786824134
E ISBN: 9781786824141

Cover artwork 'Portrait of Silbury Hill' (1989)
by David Inshaw, courtesy of Bridgeman Images

eBook conversion by Lapiz Digital Services, India.

Visit www.oberonbooks.com to read more about all our books and to buy them. You
will also find features, author interviews and news of any author events, and you can
sign up for e-newsletters so that you're always first to hear about our new releases.

Contents

Introduction

'We're not our bodies, are we, we're just in them... We're not our lives either. We're just in them. We bob about and bump into each other and our lives and our bodies slip past us.' (Edie, *Visitors*)

In these lines from *Visitors*, Edie articulates a theme that runs through all the plays in this collection: the idea of individuals adrift, buffeted by time and circumstance as they struggle to grasp and articulate a validity and purpose for their lives. What does it mean to be human? How far can we ever really connect with another person? Is it ever possible to break out of the lives we inherit? These are recurring questions in Barney Norris's work.

Fascination with the human condition shapes these plays, and the voices are authentic: these are stories that have, in every case, grown out of engagement with the communities in which they are set. Our company, Up in Arms (through which the first three plays in this collection were produced), was born out of a desire to document the lives of ordinary, unremarkable people, and give voice to those we felt were not really being heard in our theatres. The plays are patchworks, woven from the conversations, ideas and lives encountered in these communities. Through the close scrutiny of one specific strata of undocumented life, he prompts us to confront the most far-reaching questions of what it means to be alive in England today.

Visitors, the first play in this collection, is set in a farmhouse on the edge of Salisbury Plain. At its centre is a seventy year marriage – two people confronting the end of their lives and discovering that whilst there is no such thing as permanence or belonging, there is such a thing as a life-long love, and this can lend meaning to a life. Edie and Arthur are impressions of the writer's own grandparents, and the world of the play and the values of its protagonists are informed and shaped by their example. Through them, Barney paints a portrait of a way of life receding – where rootedness is set against choice, rurality against the swell of modernisation, and where, at the end of a life, there is nothing left but the love that has been shared.

'All falls away though, doesn't it. Tide goes out on us.'
(Edie, *Visitors*)

The idea of life as a series of endings is given more explicit voice in *Eventide*. Here again we find characters grappling for a way to take deliberate action in the face of a disappearing way of life. The play begins on the day that John is to hand over the keys of the local pub to a corporate chain; by the end of the play, the church – the other mainstay of village life – will see its organ replaced by a drum kit because '*the world changes.*' John philosophises on the possibility of conscious choice, and yet in the final scene – unemployed, alone and disillusioned with what he has seen of the world – he echoes Edie's expression of powerlessness:

> *'isn't it funny how time just seems to happen to you? And you never really seem to do anything except go along with it'* (John, *Eventide*)

Barney feels that as a writer he has a responsibility to document cultures before they disappear, but as a playwright he goes beyond mere reportage. What absorbs him is the human response to a changing world, and in *Eventide* we see characters cast adrift as old certainties fall away. It would be wrong, however, to regard these characters as simply symbols standing for things beyond themselves, and convenient ciphers for commenting on the human condition. *Eventide* grew out of Barney's own experience of working in a pub in a small Hampshire village, where the priorities, concerns and values seemed to be different from those in the city. Central to life there was the idea of home and of belonging somewhere. Progress, success, recognition and even money had little currency in comparison.

> *'...far as I can see, living here means keeping your head above water. Or fighting to. And failing, and moving to town, and all that breaking your heart. And no money and damp in the bedroom and taking a third or fourth job just to stay where you are, like, cos you only know this life you were born to, don't you, and you don't want to change it.'* (Mark, *Eventide*)

The duality of belonging and rootlessness is explored further through the relationship of Carol and Eddie in *While We're*

Here. This is a play that grew out of a series of visits to different communities along the South coast, homing in finally on the borough of Havant in Hampshire. Here we amassed a wealth of stories and ideas through meeting and interviewing a cross-section of the community. What emerged from these conversations and our broader excavations was a story of social isolation, of people in suburban England bumping up against the limits of their lives.

Like Mark in *Eventide* or Edie and Arthur in *Visitors,* Carol is 'hefted' – that is, she is indivisible from her home. And it is only the reappearance in her life of the restless and rootless Eddie that forces her to confront the subconscious choices she has made.

EDDIE: Did you never want to get away from this place?

CAROL: Why?

EDDIE: Don't you think you could be doing more?

CAROL: More what?

EDDIE: I don't know. I just think if you're alive in the
    world, and you're living in Havant, that's quite a
    choice you're making. You know? You can live in
    the Alps, Tuscany, Outer Mongolia. You're here.

CAROL: People are happy here.

While We're Here offers the clearest iteration of Barney's theme of individuals striving for connection. The epigraph to the play is taken from Matthew Arnold's 'To Marguerite: Continued'. Countering John Donne's oft quoted assertion, Arnold posits that every man is, in fact, an island; we are all inherently alone – aware of the sounds, shapes and movements of the other islands but never coming close enough to make contact.

> *Yes! in the sea of life enisled,*
> *With echoing straits between us thrown,*
> *Dotting the shoreless watery wild,*
> *We mortal millions live alone.*
> *The islands feel the enclasping flow,*
> *And then their endless bounds they know.*
> ('To Marguerite: Continued', Matthew Arnold)

In this way, *While We're Here* shows us two people alive to the possibility of a human connection, but unable to find the means to access it. We watch them grapple for a way to reconcile accepted truths with the offer of a different journey, until Carol is forced to concede: '*I'm walled in. I'd like to get out but I can't.*'

In *Nightfall*, the characters choose – or think they choose – to give up on the faltering past, and go in search of news lives for themselves. This seems at first like a new development, but, once again, doubts emerge over the freedom any of them exercise in turning their backs on the farm where the play unfolds. How much longer they could have stayed where they were, even if they'd wanted to, is open to question, and how much they'll change their lives by relocation is very much in doubt. The play may seem to contain more departures than the other plays in this collection, but in fact these are really the migrations forced on all of us from time to time. This family is as lost as the families that have come before them.

> '*I wanted to get away from here, that was all. After I moved back here, I thought I was going mad. I used to feel like we were waiting for something. There used to be a future. Now there isn't any more, it's now, we're in it. And there's nothing much to it.*' (Lou, *Nightfall*)

Perhaps the more significant innovation here is that, for the first time, a relationship is placed at the centre of the play where one of the two people involved has died. The distance this places between the departed father in *Nightfall*, Des, and his widow, Jenny, throws Barney's abiding questions of human connection into a different, stark relief; here, no echo ever comes back across the chasm between the two people.

There is an elegiac quality to all the plays in this collection: the world is changing, and individuals struggle to find footholds as the sands shift beneath them. Their stories are told with warmth and humanity, and human frailty is depicted with tenderness. The plays are funny too; Barney has an ear for truthful, quirky detail, and the strange way that people really talk. His work speaks eloquently of our resilience in the face of mortality, documenting the quotidian heroism at the heart of all human experience.

Alice Hamilton, March 2018

VISITORS

For my grandparents, Albert and Margaret Norris.

Man is in love and loves what vanishes,
What more is there to say?

W.B.Yeats, *Nineteen Hundred and Nineteen*

Characters

ARTHUR
about 70, a farmer

EDIE
about 70, a farmer's wife

STEPHEN
about 40, middle management in an insurance firm

KATE
20s, a university graduate

The play is set in the main room of a farm
in north Wiltshire.

Visitors was first performed at the Everyman Theatre, Cheltenham on 10 February 2014 with the following cast:

Linda Bassett – EDIE
Simon Muller – STEPHEN
Robin Soans – ARTHUR
Eleanor Wyld – KATE

Writer, Barney Norris
Director, Alice Hamilton
Designer, Francesca Reidy
Lighting Designer, Simon Gethin Thomas
Sound Designer, Frank Moon
Production Manager, Jasmine Sandalli
Stage Manager, Charlie Young
Costume Supervisor, Anouska Lester
Assistant Director, Ally Watson
Producer, Chloe Courtney
Participation Producer, Ashleigh Wheeler

The production transferred to the Bush Theatre and opened on 26 November 2014.

Linda Bassett – EDIE
Simon Muller – STEPHEN
Robin Soans – ARTHUR
Eleanor Wyld – KATE

Writer, Barney Norris
Director, Alice Hamilton
Designer, Francesca Reidy
Lighting Designer, Simon Gethin Thomas
Sound Designer, George Dennis
Production Manager, Jasmine Sandalli
Company Stage Manager, Charlie Young
Deputy Stage Manager, Josephine Rossen
Assistant Stage Manager, Rebecca Denby
Costume Supervisor, Anouska Lester
Producer, Chloe Courtney
Associate Producer, Ashleigh Wheeler

Act One

SCENE ONE

The main room of a farmhouse in north Wiltshire. EDIE and ARTHUR are sitting in chairs.

EDIE: We were having coffee on the beach. From a flask. And I had the lid and you drank straight from the nozzle. We walked there didn't we, that's the only way to get over. Up early, breakfast in the hotel, then down to the cove and up again round the cliff path till you see the second beach stretching out under you. It was cold, with the wind off the sea. We were just about warm enough in the sun but when you went into the shade…the sun was on the shingle so we thought we'd sit down. And we saw the most beautiful thing. She was all in white.

ARTHUR: Edie –

EDIE: Not now Arthur. She was all in white and in a way it was very unflashy. A simple dress almost, sheer down her sides then trailing out behind her. High neck, low back. You can do that if you have the figure. I don't think I ever did. She had the blackest hair, and such a smile. White teeth. Dark skin. The groom was just a boy. He looked too young for her. I suppose they must have been the same age. She would have better suited an older man, someone with a bit of – something about him. But you could tell they were enjoying themselves.

ARTHUR: We had a lovely wedding.

EDIE: Oh…

ARTHUR: In the church. A beautiful day. You wouldn't think it, my luck, but the sun and the trees and the church yard, 'member? They'd mowed the grass. 'Member the smell of it. Lovely day, bright in the church with the light coming

11

in through the windows. That was the happiest day of my life. I remember you coming up the aisle, and your Dad, and my heart beating that hard. When I was young I used to worry about crying at the altar. When I was a boy and imagined it, I used to be really worried I'd burst into tears. But it wasn't like that. I felt proud, and so, excited. Felt like we were getting it done.

EDIE: Then we came here. It's always been so light in the kitchen and I used to sing while I made tea in the morning, do you remember how your father hated that? He was funny. Were our lives like everyone else's? The mornings always seem so light, though they're not as bright as the middle of the day. I love how sharp the line across the garden cuts the air when you catch a sight through the kitchen window. That's the best way to dry clothes. They can't improve everything. Back then our nearest neighbours were the Joneses and the Parks. I liked the Joneses, where did they go? They had those dogs. But they were nice people. Did they have enough or go bust, which was it?

ARTHUR: Didn' mind those dogs. Meant he couldn' sneak around.

EDIE: You always knew Ted Jones was going round his yard with the barking, yes. He didn't go mad? Am I remembering – ? It was yellow wallpaper when I first came here. I did feel grown up. That was the first time I felt grown up and it was exciting, because we weren't really, were we?

ARTHUR: I used to worry before we were married. Used to worry there was something wrong with me. 'Cause I had a beautiful girl, and some days, when I didn't see you, I didn't miss you. I was happy to just get on. I could not think about you all day. You were always so pleased to see me, I used to wonder, how can I only miss her some of the time? Then I'd miss you something terrible, wouldn' be able to sleep for thinking.

EDIE: It's all right. I was the same. I didn't think about you either. I used to worry about you was all. You out there in the wheat fields and me in town with whatever errands. I worried I might not get home in time to get your tea out.

ARTHUR: Edie –

EDIE: We mustn't make a thing of today. It'll be harder for her.

ARTHUR: This might be the last time we're ever alone like this.

EDIE: No it won't. I don't know what you think's happening but it's not like that.

ARTHUR: It's just –

EDIE: She was all in white. He wasn't old enough, but they did look lovely standing in their good shoes on the shingle. There was a man in black with a camera buzzing round them. You know how flies land on bright colours? You know how cats sit on cushions? Wherever there's a cushion in a room, a cat will sit on it. That's what beauty's like, people want to be near it. The only thing that's beautiful is youth. That's when you still have your life to live, that's beautiful. That's what people are looking at when they love something. Even you and me. What I'm seeing when I look at you is the whole past, isn't it. Our lives curled round each other like ferns half furled. They're deceptive, photographs. Wedding snaps especially.

ARTHUR: Why?

EDIE: You look at a wedding photograph, it looks like the end of a story. I spose that's the books we read when we're babies. But it's not an ending, is it? It's not a start either. Just another day really.

ARTHUR: Oh.

EDIE: No, I mean, of course it's special. You know I think that. But it doesn't stop there, does it. Nothing's fixed. You have to keep working.

ARTHUR: Oh, I see. Oh yes. You have to keep on.

EDIE: He should be here by now. Is that clock right?

ARTHUR: Wound it up this morning so we'd know when they'd arrive.

EDIE: I wish she'd just come and we could get the first cup of tea out the way.

ARTHUR: Feels like an ending an all. Doesn't it come quick? Whoosh! Was that it? Yup, that was your life mate. How long do you think we've got?

EDIE: Oh, don't. I've got longer than you have.

ARTHUR: Oh, you –

EDIE: We used to laugh, didn't we? You used to say you'll never catch me up.

ARTHUR: You won't, you know. I've still got years on you. My young thing.

EDIE: If I could choose any life I don't think I'd have things very different from this. These chairs are very comfortable. Do you get tired sitting up? I've got you, and you make me laugh. Perhaps if I could have been a despot and lived without a thought for anyone else. What are their names, the very bad ones? It must have been blissful to be Pol Pot or Hitler, they could do what they wanted, they were mad, it didn't matter to them. They could have made the shops open later just like that. I suppose we're all mad aren't we, they just got to show it off. But I've enjoyed all this.

ARTHUR: I would have liked to have experienced the sixties.

EDIE: Well you were alive in them.

ARTHUR: I mean I would have liked to have tried LSD.

EDIE: We still could, you know, they still make it. Shall we get some? Would you have liked free love?

ARTHUR: I wouldn't have got any and you would have got loads.

EDIE: There won't be as much of that now we've got company.

ARTHUR: Ho ho.

EDIE: Do you miss that? Sexual love?

ARTHUR: Yes.

EDIE: Yes. We could try that. Nights when she's out. Bit of romantic lighting. How long did we plan for that holiday? Half my life it seems we talked. All I remember's you complaining about the price of parking.

ARTHUR: Oh my love, I'm sorry.

EDIE: I'm joking, aren't I.

ARTHUR: I've been selfish to you all my life.

EDIE: No you weren't, shut up.

ARTHUR: I was.

EDIE: Don't let's talk about big things now.

ARTHUR: When can I?

EDIE: I don't know. Not today.

ARTHUR: Look – I never could argue with you.

EDIE: You always tried. You'd get so cross because you never had an answer. You'd go out to the shed to sulk.

ARTHUR: I get a lot done in that shed.

EDIE: I know you did, love. You've always been good at mending.

ARTHUR: Anyone can fix anything with a bit of care, I wasn't special. Patient.

EDIE: You had a knack.

ARTHUR: Practice.

EDIE: Don't be modest. I've always been proud.

ARTHUR: Didn't you mind?

EDIE: What?

ARTHUR: That everything was mended. We didn't buy much new. I always fixed things, but I used to think maybe things broke for a reason. Maybe we'd rather a new thing. All those women, your friends, used to go on about their machines, their sofas. We never did. I fixed the old ones. Did you feel left out? Would you have preferred it if I'd spent a bit more money? I don't want to have been tight. Did I come across as tight-fisted?

EDIE: Oh my love.

ARTHUR: Does that mean I was or I wasn't?

EDIE: Of course you weren't. Besides, we bought things. All the new electronics. When I wanted a dishwasher we got one, didn't we?

ARTHUR: But was the house dowdy, did you think that?

EDIE: You worry too much. I thought it looked like us. What'll happen after us, d'you think?

ARTHUR: Some stranger will live here.

EDIE: I suppose it's for the best.

ARTHUR: I used to hope the boy'd change his mind. But he's all set up, isn't he. We took too long.

EDIE: Don't talk soft. We'll take a while yet. We've ten years in us. Twenty.

ARTHUR: Christ, imagine that.

EDIE: You do make me laugh. My love. We could lay traps for whoever lives here after.

ARTHUR: What do you mean?

EDIE: False floorboards. Alarm clocks hidden in the walls. Make them believe in ghosts. Look at this.

She gets up, crosses the room, stands on a creaky board.

EDIE: We could make everything make noises like that. Would it be possible to rig a cupboard door in such a way that every time you opened it, something happened to the toaster? Could you do that?

ARTHUR: Maybe.

EDIE: Or a window swing open. Or every time the window swings open for the door to close. I'd love that.

She neatens the room.

ARTHUR: It was so quiet, wasn't it. You could have sat there all day, if you could only keep warm. And watch the light changing through Durdle Door as if you looked into another world. Sit and do nothing. It would be wonderful to live like that.

EDIE: If I could have just one day again with my old legs and my old vitality and know while I had it how precious it was. I wouldn't do anything special, you know I never liked cake or rollercoasters or anything, maybe the seaside, nothing particular. I just didn't know how fast it would all get behind me.

She sits down.

ARTHUR: Do you think a lot of people have heart attacks at Lulworth Cove? Walking up that chalk path over the hill? I should think it's a hazard of the landscape.

EDIE: It's all right Arthur. You don't have to be frightened. It's just us two talking together.

ARTHUR: Edie.

EDIE: Don't be scared.

ARTHUR: I think in a way it's better never to live by the sea at all than live by the sea and have to put up with a shingle beach.

EDIE: Do you think I could have got away with a dress like that?

ARTHUR: You would have put her to shame. My young thing.

A knock at the door.

ARTHUR: That'll be her. *(Shouts.)* It's open, come in! Hello? We won't get up, come in!

EDIE: Will that be Stephen?

ARTHUR: He wouldn't knock. He hasn't come in time. Hello?

EDIE: Arthur.

ARTHUR: Can you hear me? Open the door and come in!

EDIE: Arthur?

ARTHUR: Yes love?

EDIE: You were just right.

ARTHUR: You what love?

EDIE: Just right.

ARTHUR: Oh God.

He gets up.

ARTHUR: Come in!

KATE enters.

KATE: I hope you don't mind, I let myself / in.

ARTHUR: Oh dear.

ARTHUR falls.

KATE: Oh my / God. Are you all right?

EDIE: Arthur? Arthur?

ARTHUR: I'm all right.

KATE: Don't get up on your own.

EDIE: Arthur?

ARTHUR: Timbeeer!

KATE: Can you get up? All right? That's good.

EDIE: Arthur?

ARTHUR: I'm all right. Whoo!

KATE: Back in the chair.

ARTHUR: Yep. Yep.

EDIE: Arthur?

ARTHUR: Didn't you hear me? I was shouting.

KATE: I'm sorry, I couldn't –

ARTHUR: It's fine. Edie, are you all right?

KATE: Should I –

ARTHUR: Wait a second. Are you all right Edie?

EDIE: Just right.

ARTHUR: I'm sorry about that. You're Kate, then?

KATE: Yes. Listen I'm so / sorry –

ARTHUR: Edie, are you all right?

EDIE: Just tired.

ARTHUR: That's all right. I'm sorry. Right. Why don't you take a seat and we can all calm down?

KATE: OK.

ARTHUR: No, would you do something for me? Could you get us all a cup of tea? It's good for a scare.

KATE: OK.

ARTHUR: The kitchen's through there. She doesn't take sugar and I take four.

KATE: OK.

ARTHUR: There's not an electric kettle so you boil it on the AGA.

KATE: That's fine.

ARTHUR: Thank you. I'd like to make it for you but I feel shook up.

KATE: Do you want me to call a doctor? Are you sure you're all right?

ARTHUR: Just through there.

KATE: OK.

KATE goes into the kitchen. ARTHUR gets up and goes to EDIE.

ARTHUR: There you go. Did I scare you? I'm sorry. You know where you are?

EDIE: I'm all right. You gave me a fright.

ARTHUR: Imagine how I feel. I'm going to sit down.

EDIE: Do you mind if I just have a rest?

ARTHUR: Of course. You sit back. All right? All right.

ARTHUR straightens.

ARTHUR: Working all day but I can't get out of an armchair now?

EDIE: Comes and goes, doesn't it.

ARTHUR: Apparently so.

Enter KATE.

KATE: Oh Mr Wakeling, you're out of your chair.

ARTHUR: That's very astute of you, yes. I thought I would reassure you that I'm not in fact an infirm old bastard, by sitting down unaided. *(He does so.)* There. I'm sorry we've met in – inauspicious circumstances. We were having a good day till you got here. Not that you – I only mean, call me Arthur. We're Arthur and Edie, you don't have to call me Mr Wakeling. I had the misfortune to be born with a surname made me sound like a cake.

EDIE: I don't know what I was thinking when I married him. My name was Wardley, it was perfectly nice. I might have been a nice old maid with more time for my lacework.

KATE: The kettle's on. It's got one of those singing –

ARTHUR: Do you want to sit down till it does?

KATE: Yeah, sure.

ARTHUR: I'm sorry my son's not here, he wanted to be here before you. You've met before though?

KATE: Yes, he met me last week. I'm sorry I'm only meeting you now. There's normally a thing first, but I was away.

ARTHUR: No bother. We figured you're all signed up, someone must think you're all right. Steve said you were all right. I just hope you think we're all right, is all.

EDIE: Pair of wrung out funny old dishcloths is us.

ARTHUR: Yes. Well. We don't get a lot of visitors out here, it's a red letter – been fun planning. You know? Having to fit in with a – yes. Well. Where have you been then while you were away?

KATE: I was WWOOFING.

ARTHUR: You what?

KATE: It's an acronym for a travel thing. Working on organic farms. It's this network of farms that put you up all over Europe if you do a bit of work.

ARTHUR: I didn't know they were sending us a farmer.

KATE: Well –

ARTHUR: We're not an organic farm. Nothing bad, just pesticides an that for killing the insects.

EDIE: And the moles.

ARTHUR: And the moles of course, we do them with traps.

EDIE: Snap!

KATE: I was really happy when I found out where you lived.

ARTHUR: Did you grow up on a farm, or –

KATE: No, I'm new to it. But I loved it.

ARTHUR: See if you're saying that after fifty years.

EDIE: Oh –

KATE: Have you always farmed?

ARTHUR: I've been here all my life.

KATE: In this house?

ARTHUR: Family farm. My father and his father before him.

KATE: That's amazing.

ARTHUR: Well. Where were you when you were farming?

KATE: I went round France. Lots of time around Clermont-Ferrand.

ARTHUR: I don't know France.

KATE: It's nice. It's better coming back to England.

ARTHUR: Oh yes. Will you go again next year?

KATE: I don't think so. It's tiring, isn't it, fields.

ARTHUR: I can't help but notice that you have blue hair.

EDIE: I had both hands wrapped round this thermos flask lid that stayed absolutely cool even though the drink in it was hot, and the steam from the coffee rising up. You're only really meant to drink it in the morning. And we saw this woman who was so very beautiful. She was getting married on the beach, they must have had a special licence. They were playing the Beach Boys on a portable cassette player. *(She sings 'God Only Knows', wordlessly.)*

ARTHUR: I should say now, Edie's not always able to keep up with a conversation. That's one of the things, why Steve's got you in.

EDIE: When we were first married I thought we'd have so many children, boys and girls. I think it's a shame there was only Stephen in the end.

ARTHUR: She remembers some things very clearly. Other things she finds hard.

KATE: I see.

ARTHUR: It's not something to be scared around. The thing to do is talk to her.

EDIE: I feel tired, Arthur.

ARTHUR: I know love, we'll get you upstairs soon. When her mother was dying she was the same. Not that Edie's – it's just similar, you know. But her mother was getting worse and worse, except when Edie used to read her a book. In between books her mind was unspooling, but when there was something to hold her attention –

KATE: I know the thing you mean, yeah.

EDIE: And it's very sad but we learn to get on with it.

ARTHUR: We were happy when Steve read about your thing on the internet, it'll make everything nicer having someone here.

EDIE: We have been to France, Arthur.

ARTHUR: I know. But the north, not to Clermont –

KATE: Ferrand.

EDIE: It was only a channel hop. But when I was forty we went to France. On the ferry.

KATE: Oh yeah?

EDIE: Have you ever heard of a catamaran?

KATE: Yeah, I have, yeah.

EDIE: Do they still have them?

KATE: I think so. I've never been on one.

EDIE: Oh, holidays are wonderful, you should go on as many holidays as you can. They float on top of the water.

ARTHUR: Catamarans.

EDIE: Shut up, she knows. They float on the water like skimming a stone. But you can take your car and everything.

KATE: Oh yeah?

EDIE: I don't know why he's acting superior. He was sick into the wind and it went all over him.

ARTHUR: I wasn't very good at the catamaran.

EDIE: Arthur doesn't like a journey, he likes to stay at home. I like looking forward to something.

ARTHUR: I have to stay at home, I've got a farm to run.

KATE: Holidays, you mean?

EDIE: Well, anything really. I don't think there'll be a lot more holidays for me.

KATE: You never know.

EDIE: I can be relatively confident. When you were a child where did you go when you went away?

KATE: Oh, loads of places I guess.

EDIE: You didn't have one house you'd always go to?

KATE: We used to go a lot to the same bit of Devon. Not really the same house.

ARTHUR: More of a caravan girl?

EDIE: Arthur! He thinks caravans are for the working class.

ARTHUR: How can I, I am working class, I work all the time.

EDIE: Yes, but we own all our furniture.

KATE: We did do a bit of caravanning.

EDIE: Oh yes?

KATE: It was – pretty chavvy, yeah. But you don't notice at the time, do you.

EDIE: I suppose they're comfortable inside. And what did you do before you were in France?

KATE: I was at uni. In Scotland.

EDIE: Oh yes? And what did you study?

KATE: Law.

EDIE: Really?

KATE: Yeah. It was good. It's hard to get work, but. I mean I don't know how I'll ever do anything with it. It was a good time though.

EDIE: And what is it you want to do then? After you're done with this kind of thing?

KATE: You mean –

EDIE: If you're looking after farms one year and the elderly the next, and you won't be a lawyer, what's it all with a view to?

The kettle starts to sing.

KATE: That's the kettle. I'd better get the tea.

ARTHUR: Thank you.

KATE: I won't be a moment.

EDIE: All right love.

KATE exits.

ARTHUR: Be nice to her, all right?

EDIE: What did I say?

ARTHUR: She probably doesn't know what she wants to do.

EDIE: Maybe she wants to do this.

ARTHUR: Hardly anyone thinks they're doing what they want to, do they?

EDIE: That's the saddest thing about you that you think that.

Enter KATE.

KATE: One with none one with four.

EDIE: Arthur.

ARTHUR: Well –

KATE: He won't have it every time.

ARTHUR: I am here, you know.

EDIE: You won't be for long if you put that much sugar in your tea.

ARTHUR: All right, all right. So tell us, Kate. What does your father do?

KATE: Well my Mum's a dinner lady.

ARTHUR: In a school?

KATE: Yeah, a primary school. I'm not in touch with my Dad.

ARTHUR: Me and Steve have been a bit hit and miss over the years.

KATE: Actually I've never known my Dad. We don't know who he is.

ARTHUR: Where is Steve anyway? He was supposed to get here before you.

KATE: It was really kind of him to meet me last week.

ARTHUR: Kind doesn't come into it, he wanted the day away.

EDIE: Arthur.

ARTHUR: His interest is himself, he doesn't really care for other people. He'd put you away if he could afford it.

EDIE: Arthur!

ARTHUR: Thing is, he can't. There's no money to show for all the work we've done. Steve moved away to make more of himself, but he hasn't really. I'm not trying to be cruel. I just mean he hasn't made much more money than he might have if he'd stayed with us. Life insurance. Seems a stupid business. You always pay out, don't you? Everyone always dies.

EDIE: That's not kind Arthur. He's a wonderful boy. And some people don't get their payouts if their policies lapse. Didn't you think he was a wonderful boy?

KATE: Well –

EDIE: He's always been good hearted. But didn't you like him? He's hard to get on with, but you liked him, didn't you?

KATE: Yeah –

ARTHUR: I've been cruel, haven't I? I'm sorry, I'd planned this conversation so you'd think we were all right but it's not going quite how I wanted.

EDIE: That's what happens to me.

KATE: Oh yes?

EDIE: Imagine I was a gardener. And I'd decided to pack all the gardening in. I don't know, maybe I couldn't be bothered. Maybe my back was gone. Well some of the paths get overgrown, so I can't walk down them. But some are still open, so I walk down them instead. And they're so unfamiliar, I haven't been down them in years. I'll try to tell Arthur about my day and all I can think is the way he threw up on the catamaran and I ended up sponging him clean, as if he were dough I were kneading. You know?

KATE: Right.

EDIE: I don't think you do. It's hard to explain. What you want to say builds up like water behind a dam but the dam will never open again. You talk about the past when you mean to ask for the butter knife. Or when you talk about little things what you think of is the things you love, and you want to talk about them, but the words won't come. And they will never come again. The best thing about having you here will be help in the kitchen.

KATE: Yes?

EDIE: I don't trust myself any more with the electric bread knife, and sometimes when I'm draining the potatoes, I say to myself do you know what, this is too heavy for you, you're going to drop this. I find if you say that it tends to buy you a bit of time.

KATE: Well I can help in the kitchen.

EDIE: We don't need help in the bathroom.

ARTHUR: Unless we get stuck in the bath.

EDIE: I have a way of getting up the stairs that's about swinging myself up on my arms, and it looks a bit dangerous, but you mustn't worry. Sometimes if I'm tired I find it easier to go down the stairs one by one on my backside, but you mustn't worry about that either. I think everyone would go down stairs like that if they didn't think it looked funny.

KATE: Right.

EDIE: We get up very early and go to bed early because we don't sleep well. Things have to have a routine because that's going to be good for me as I get worse. We sleep in different rooms because we keep each other up. Most days we're not as odd as you've found us, today is a red letter day because you're arriving and it's a bit more excitement than we're used to so we're talking too much.

ARTHUR: We'll talk less once we've calmed down.

KATE: You're not talking too much.

ARTHUR: I suppose it feels a lot because we hardly talk at all on an ordinary day. I think we're both worried you've changed your mind and you're thinking of leaving.

KATE: I'm not. I'm excited to be here.

ARTHUR: How long are you planning to stay?

EDIE: Oh, Arthur –

KATE: No, it's important you have some idea. So – honestly – well you asked me what I wanted to do. And the thing is, I'm not quite sure at the moment. Cos the thing with me, the thing is I'm just a bit mad. I finished school, and went to uni, and that was all great, but now there isn't really anything for me, and there's nothing I want to – go after, either. So I went round France because I wanted to take some time out and it sounded like fun, but you can't actually take time out of your life, can you, you're just losing time. So I'd signed up for this programme before I left, this homeshare thing, so for as long as I don't know what I want to do eventually, I'm happy to be here. Because it feels like I'm helpful. So I was thinking I'd stay for a while?

ARTHUR: It's been such a change in our lifetime, how people fix up their lives. For me and Edie, I don't think it entered our heads we'd do anything very different to this. It's what we were born to, isn't it. Then for Steve when he left, my son decided he didn't want to farm you see, you've met him haven't you, and that was a big choice, that was deciding to break with something. That was a big fight we had then. But in the end we thought, that's probably what progress looks like, because he can have a better life now. And perhaps he has. Now to hear you talk it's like it's changed again.

KATE: How?

ARTHUR: There's no question you might do anything other than go off looking for a life for yourself. That you might inherit anything.

KATE: I suppose not.

ARTHUR: I don't mean things, I mean your life.

KATE: I know what you mean.

ARTHUR: I suppose you're much freer.

KATE: Maybe, yeah.

EDIE: Opportunity. Much more is possible, it's wonderful really.

KATE: Yes.

ARTHUR: I wonder what you lose. Do you think you have to fight for things, do you think that still happens?

KATE: I don't know. I find everything difficult, but that might just be me.

ARTHUR: Causes, that's what used to be possible to come by. The Worker's Alliance Party. People used to aspire to things. Does that still happen?

KATE: Sort of. There's a lot of aspiring. I don't know what to.

ARTHUR: I suppose that's what happens when everyone finally gets a bit of money. After the war –

EDIE: Oh –

ARTHUR: There was nothing, you had to really want a thing to get it. You wouldn't believe it now. There was nothing, there was nothing, there was no string, nothing. We used to save paper bags on a nail over that fireplace. You can't describe it. I was hardly born. But I remember.

EDIE: She was all in white, and in a way it was very unflashy. A sheer dress, almost, straight down her body then flowing out like champagne overflowing the banks of a glass.

The clock strikes four.

ARTHUR: How is your tea?

KATE: Fine thanks.

ARTHUR: Steve was meant to be here an hour ago.

KATE: Probably traffic.

ARTHUR: Over Salisbury Plain? When he got here I was planning to properly settle you in. Show you the house and where you'd be sleeping. He's ruined it now, I feel like you've come in all backwards.

KATE: It's fine, really.

ARTHUR: I should have made the tea as well, I'm sorry, I wanted to check Edie. But she was all right and I should have made the tea.

EDIE: Of course I was.

ARTHUR: You're not always.

KATE: Mr Wakeling, it's fine. Don't worry. I know it's a bit weird me coming here. It's a bit weird for me too. It's all right if it's awkward.

ARTHUR: I thought we could all have dinner together, the four of us later.

KATE: That'd be lovely.

ARTHUR: You don't have to eat with us every day. We want you to treat this place as your own, and live how you want as much as possible. It's only if we need you we'll ask for anything.

KATE: Thank you.

ARTHUR: Will you be all right?

KATE: What do you mean?

ARTHUR: Well what worries us is we're out in the middle of nowhere. Will you be all right living here? There's not much in the way of fun.

KATE: This is what I'm looking for. A bit of quiet.

EDIE: It's the wrong time in your life to be looking for that.

KATE: Maybe.

ARTHUR: You have to tell us if you start to go mad, because we don't want to be trouble. Steve gave me the papers about this programme you're on, it seemed to me most of the kids who did it went to cities, part of the attraction was finding somewhere cheap to live in London or – Manchester. Did you not want that?

EDIE: We didn't think we'd find anyone, you know.

KATE: No?

EDIE: We advertised and you were the only person who replied.

ARTHUR: You're not on the run or anything, are you?

KATE: What from?

EDIE: He's joking. You're not in hiding from the police or something stupid?

KATE: Oh, no. Nothing like that.

EDIE: That's all right then.

ARTHUR: Not that we thought you might be. It was just a little joke we had. I feel like this has all gone wrong.

KATE: Really, it hasn't. It's great.

EDIE: You make a good cup of tea.

KATE: I'm glad.

ARTHUR: Well I'm glad we've got all that sorted out. It's important to arrange things, isn't it. I'm glad we've had this chat.

EDIE: When I was a young woman and hadn't met Arthur I used to imagine my husband. Did you used to do that?

KATE: All the time, yeah.

EDIE: How did you see him?

KATE: I don't know really. I thought he'd be tall. Mysterious, maybe.

EDIE: Then when you got older you got interested in other things about him.

KATE: Yeah, I guess so. By then I was trying them out though.

EDIE: Husbands?

KATE: Boys, yeah.

EDIE: I never had a chance for that.

KATE: No?

ARTHUR: Get in early, that was my plan.

EDIE: Oh –

ARTHUR: We met very young.

KATE: How old?

EDIE: I was eleven and he was thirteen.

KATE: Cheeky.

EDIE: Nothing happened for a long time.

ARTHUR: A very long time.

EDIE: My Dad was the groundsman of the golf course, and Arthur was poaching in the wood at the edge. So one day I was walking in the woods with my friend, and we caught him passing the other way with a trout under his arm.

ARTHUR: Ticklin' em up.

EDIE: I knew what he was doing, and I said excuse me, this is my father's golf course, what do you think you're doing walking over it? And he said –

ARTHUR: I'm the postman!

EDIE: Then he ran off.

KATE: Cheeky!

ARTHUR: Good fish that.

KATE: Did you have your eye on her from then, then?

ARTHUR: Oh yeah. Only took, what, seven more years after that?

EDIE: I never told on him so I think I must have liked him even then. He was an idiot at school.

ARTHUR: I never tried at school, I knew what I was doing after.

EDIE: I remember being like you though.

KATE: Like me?

EDIE: At the start of everything. And you're unsure because you could be anyone, really, and you don't know which life to have. When you're our age you feel unsure because you don't know whether you did it as well as you could have.

ARTHUR: And you haven't really.

EDIE: There are days and days you can't remember, after all. But the worst is in between you and me, to be Stephen, in your life, set on your course, and just not sure whether you're doing it right.

STEPHEN: *(Off.)* Hello!

ARTHUR: That's Steve. You won't say I fell, will you?

KATE: Really?

ARTHUR: Please don't.

KATE: I can't –

Enter STEPHEN.

STEPHEN: Sorry I'm late.

SCENE TWO

EDIE: What was – I'm in the park and he's coming to give me my birthday present. We're meeting on my lunch, I'm still at school and he's left, you see. What was – I sit on a bench near the school entrance to the park, just the other side of this hedge from the main gate, that's where everyone goes to have a cigarette. But I wasn't there for a fag. Why had I – ? Oh yes. He comes in the park and he has this bag and I know it's full of things for me, he's bringing me all these things he thinks I'll like for my birthday. It's very sweet, he's like a little dog. When a cat brings you a mouse. I watch him crossing the park

35

and that right there is a moment when – what is it? Well I knew for sure anyway, I felt so big with the feeling. What was it? He gets to me and we both sit down. But we can't have had a cup of tea. I don't think we'd gone to a tea shop. Oh, no. We were in a park. And that was a favourite place of ours, we used to lie down in there, I let him be very fast. I didn't worry, because I knew. What was I – ? I can see him walking in and out of the light across the park with his face sometimes dappled and his face sometimes clear. I wish I could put my finger on it. Put a pin in my life and say, this is the moment I became myself. This is the scene my life was about. Can I go now? Can I go? Can I go now? I need the toilet.

Enter STEPHEN, carrying a dish cloth, drying his hands.

STEPHEN: All right old crone?

EDIE: Yes.

STEPHEN: Do you need the loo?

EDIE: No, it's the only way is all.

STEPHEN: Only way what?

EDIE: If I just call you don't come. You'll only look after me if I threaten to pee on the armchairs.

STEPHEN: How are you feeling?

EDIE: Did you like your tea?

STEPHEN: I loved it.

EDIE: Did you?

STEPHEN: I did, I loved it.

EDIE: Do you cook at home?

STEPHEN: Sometimes. Emily does most of the cooking.

EDIE: She's a good cook is she?

STEPHEN: Great.

EDIE: I've begun a project in the kitchen.

STEPHEN: Oh yeah?

EDIE: I don't cook all the old things any more. I threw Constance Spry away. I'm learning to cook new dishes.

STEPHEN: Like what?

EDIE: Oh, anything really. I buy new cook books. Yotam Ottolenghi. A cook book from London I tried to learn falafels out of.

STEPHEN: Falafels, Mum.

EDIE: Is it? I thought it was falafels. Anyway, they were impossible. Flour and beans, we got past that in the fifties.

STEPHEN: I like falafels.

EDIE: You should try mine. Your Dad wouldn't touch them.

STEPHEN: I would have loved them, I bet they were marvellous.

EDIE: I think you are like a psychopath, because you're very charming.

STEPHEN: Why does that make me a psychopath?

EDIE: Psychopaths are charming. And I don't want to be mad on my own.

STEPHEN: You're not mad, Mum.

EDIE: That's what it feels like, going mad. I've seen people further down the line than me. They reach for words. They'll point at a glass of water and say 'can you pass me the – the the the the / the the...'

STEPHEN: All right, not now Mum yeah? Let's not think about that right now.

EDIE: I'm only messing about.

STEPHEN: It's harder for us, you know.

EDIE: It's not.

STEPHEN: It will be eventually. You won't know your arse from your elbow and we'll still be in love with you, won't we.

EDIE: I couldn't love anyone who thought their elbows were their –

STEPHEN: No, well. What do you think of her?

EDIE: Who?

STEPHEN: Kate.

EDIE: Who?

STEPHEN: Kate, Mum, the girl we – at dinner – are you joking?

EDIE: Course I am.

STEPHEN: Mum!

EDIE: I'd forgotten her name, I knew she was here though.

STEPHEN: Thank God for that.

EDIE: God's got nothing to do with it.

STEPHEN: Sorry. You can say Thank God if you mean it can't you?

EDIE: Yes, but you don't mean it.

STEPHEN: Mother! Do you like her?

EDIE: She seems nice.

STEPHEN: But she's such a good idea, isn't she? She's going to be such a help?

EDIE: I'm sure she is.

STEPHEN: You must be a bit pleased.

EDIE: I'm sorry Steve, I am pleased.

STEPHEN: You have to accept / Dad's got to be out and you –

EDIE: I do.

Enter KATE.

KATE: All done.

STEPHEN: We were just talking about you.

KATE: Yeah?

EDIE: He thinks I'm not pleased enough.

STEPHEN: Mum.

KATE: Aren't you?

EDIE: Oh, I'm happy, of course I'm happy. I just wonder about dying, don't I.

STEPHEN: Mum.

KATE: That's natural.

EDIE: I know. He doesn't, but you and I do.

KATE: That's why we'll get on. We can wonder about dying together.

EDIE: I don't think it need concern you yet.

KATE: I get so obsessed though. Last year, I was reading this poem and you know? I just suddenly knew with this amazing – certainty, that I was going to die. I mean, definitely die. I freaked man, I didn't sleep for weeks after. I couldn't believe it.

STEPHEN: You always knew it was going to happen though?

KATE: Yeah. But I never knew knew, you know?

STEPHEN: Hardest two questions my girls have asked me. First was, where do we go when we die?

EDIE: Oh yes.

STEPHEN: You can't believe it when they ask you! It happens so young.

KATE: How old were they?

STEPHEN: Hannah was four or five or something? So I'm twenty – what? I'm in my twenties. And this kid comes up to you and asks, where do we go when we die? Well I don't know, do I. And I've had no advice on what you're meant to say when that happens. That's not in the baby manuals! If you're, if you're like me and you think there's nothing –

EDIE: Oh –

STEPHEN: Sorry Mum – if you think there's nothing then isn't it your moral – obligation to say that? Otherwise you're going to have to lie to this child and later they're going to know you lied to them. But if you say to a child, there's nothing after you die, your life just ends, aren't you going to freak her out? So Hannah asks me and all this is rushing through my head and I'm thinking, what's the youngest ever recorded suicide? It's like, Jude the Obscure isn't it? Could you do that to a kid if you tell her there's nothing after death? And then you start thinking, what if I'm wrong? Do I have a right to rule out the possibility of faith in this kid's life? I've hardly ever been right about anything. What if I'm wrong and she thinks there's no point in being good and misbehaves all her life and then she dies and it turns out there is a heaven, and she has to go to hell because I told her there was no point in behaving?

KATE: What did you say?

STEPHEN: I was so confused, I just said, I don't know. And Hannah nodded, she looked really serious and said, I see. So I thought, great, she's fallen for that as an actual answer. So I got into it a bit and I said, I don't think we can know. And she said great, thanks Dad. And then she walked off.

KATE: So you have two / daughters?

STEPHEN: Yeah. Hannah and Sam. Samantha, we all call her Sam. She insists.

EDIE: And she gets what she wants!

STEPHEN: They're growing up now, fifteen and thirteen, they're impossible. D'you wanna see a picture?

KATE: Sure.

EDIE: Have you got a picture?

STEPHEN: Yeah.

EDIE: Can I see it too?

STEPHEN: Of course, sorry, of course.

EDIE: Oh, lovely. Don't they look lovely. Doesn't Hannah look like her mother now?

STEPHEN: Scowling.

EDIE: Will of her own.

STEPHEN: Mum and Emily don't get on.

EDIE: Why would you tell her that? What have I said?

STEPHEN: Will of her own? Come off it. I'm just explaining why you went all –

EDIE: There's nothing to explain. Emma's just –

STEPHEN: Emily.

EDIE: That's right.

KATE: Here's your –

STEPHEN: Thanks.

EDIE: She's got a will of her own is all, she's a strong woman.

KATE: So Hannah's doing her GCSEs?

STEPHEN: Just started, yeah. It's so strange. You remember doing them yourself, you know?

KATE: Yeah.

EDIE: GCSEs were yesterday for her.

KATE: Well, six years.

STEPHEN: I did O levels.

EDIE: What did the O stand for?

STEPHEN: God knows.

KATE: Are they at the same school?

STEPHEN: No. Hannah got into the grammar, Sam didn't, so she goes to the comp. It's hard. I don't think Sam cares. Yet. Hannah does. And we do.

KATE: Yeah?

STEPHEN: We stayed where we are because of the grammar school. Otherwise we might have lived anywhere, we both do work that could happen pretty much anywhere.

KATE: What do you – ?

STEPHEN: I'm in insurance. Emily works down in Southampton, at the university.

KATE: She's an academic?

STEPHEN: No, administrative work. So we feel like the girls going to different schools is our fault really.

KATE: What's the other hardest question you've been asked?

EDIE: Oh, that's the obvious.

KATE: What?

EDIE: Where do babies come from.

STEPHEN: Yeah.

KATE: Oh right.

STEPHEN: Where do babies come from Daddy? Can I have one? Can I have one, she said.

KATE: How old?

STEPHEN: Hannah was – five or six, I guess. She worked out dying before she worked out sex. I don't know whether that's good or bad.

EDIE: What a strange question.

KATE: What did you say?

STEPHEN: Well I knew you were supposed to start with, 'when a man and a woman love each other very much'. So I said that. And then I thought, I've never heard this speech. Dad never did it. I didn't know what you were meant to say next. I mean, what do you actually say? So I said, they get together and make a baby.

EDIE: And then it grows in the Mummy's tummy and when it's ready it comes out.

STEPHEN: Yeah. It was so scary. There was a second where I really was about to say to my five-year-old child, when a man and a woman love each other very much they fuck each other.

EDIE: Potty mouth.

STEPHEN: Sorry Mum.

EDIE: Your language is appalling / Stephen.

STEPHEN: Mum thinks saying God or Jesus is swearing.

EDIE: I don't think it is, I know it is! It is swearing!

STEPHEN: Sorry.

EDIE: That's enough of this. I'd like to go to bed.

STEPHEN: I was only –

EDIE: It's all right. Will you help me up?

KATE: I'll help you.

STEPHEN: I don't mind –

KATE: Why don't we get into the habit?

EDIE: Are you sure?

KATE: I'd like to.

EDIE: Well thank you. Is the washing up done?

KATE: Yeah. Come on, show me where your room is.

EDIE: All right.

STEPHEN: Thanks.

EDIE: Night Steve, love to the girls.

STEPHEN: Night Mum.

Enter ARTHUR.

ARTHUR: That's the chickens in.

EDIE: Have you locked up the chickens?

ARTHUR: Just done. Sly buggers.

EDIE: They are, they are.

ARTHUR: Off to bed?

EDIE: Yes.

ARTHUR: Is Kate going to take you?

KATE: Is that all right?

EDIE: Of course it is, he's just talking to me like I'm a baby.

ARTHUR: I'm not!

EDIE: You are, that was baby talk. You patronise me now I'm going senile.

ARTHUR: Well you patronised me all my life.

EDIE: I did not. I just talked very slowly because you're thick.

ARTHUR: All right. Night you.

EDIE: Good night love.

KATE: Down in a minute.

Exit KATE and EDIE.

STEPHEN: Good dinner, right?

ARTHUR: Oh, yeah? Cous cous. I mean, really. I've never known anything took longer to get through or gave less pleasure.

STEPHEN: She likes it.

ARTHUR: Mediterranean stuffed peppers. Waste of cheese. I hate running round like that in that yard.

STEPHEN: You shouldn't keep chickens.

ARTHUR: Your mother likes them.

STEPHEN: Yeah.

ARTHUR: What?

STEPHEN: She won't want them much longer, will she?

ARTHUR: Right.

ARTHUR starts to rearrange and tidy the furniture.

STEPHEN: Wanna hear a joke?

ARTHUR: What?

STEPHEN: Wanna hear a joke?

ARTHUR: Go on then.

STEPHEN: This old bloke dies, and he gets to the pearly gates and St Paul says sorry mate, we're full up, have to try the other place. So he goes to hell, and Satan meets him at the door and says come on in, always room for one more! So he gets ushered in, and Satan takes his coat and says, actually, this is your lucky day, we've been trialling a new customer-oriented management model here, because we're so uncompetitive in terms of attracting guests and our board really don't see why everyone in the history of the world should always want to go to the room upstairs. So you've still come to hell, but that doesn't have to be the worst news you've ever had, oh no. We're putting people's fates back in their own hands. Today I'm going to give you a choice of how you'd like to spend the rest of eternity, because our board know that customers value choice. That's the lesson of the free market – choice, choice, choice, and when we did our market research we found there was nothing on earth people associated more closely with Satan than the free market. Except perhaps genocide. But I'm quite busy today, we've got a lot of new visitors, so if it's all right with you I'll give you a choice of three. So the bloke says, OK, sounds good, lead on Macduff. So Satan opens a grille in a door and shows him a room. In the room, there's a lake of fire with men drowning in it. Your standard model, he says, pretty average day in hell. Bloke says OK, what's next? And in the next room he sees lots of blokes strapped to rocks having their stomachs eaten by vultures and then growing back to be eaten again. Bit of a classical reference, Satan says, for the sophisticated sufferer. Bloke nods, he'd like to see the last one please. And in the third room, he sees a lot of men standing around waist-deep in shit, sipping coffee. They've all got little cups of coffee, with little saucers, and they're in like a swimming pool of shit. There's a devil imp lifeguard at one end, and all these blokes just standing around. So the bloke says this one looks much better, I'll do this! I mean, it smells, but it's better than fire or getting eaten alive, and you get something to drink. So Satan shows him in, says have a nice afterlife, and the bloke stands in the shit with the others. It's a bit squelchy, it stinks, but he thinks, I have so won here, this is much better. Then suddenly a whistle goes. And the little lifeguard imp says right, break's over, see you in five hundred years – back on your heads!

ARTHUR: St Peter.

STEPHEN: What?

ARTHUR: It's St Peter guards the pearly gates. 'And I will give unto thee the keys of the kingdom of heaven: and whatsoever thou shalt bind on earth shall be bound in heaven: and whatsoever thou shalt loose on earth shall be loosed in heaven.' Matthew 16:19.

STEPHEN: Right.

ARTHUR: You staying?

STEPHEN: I've got to get back.

Silence.

Act Two

SCENE ONE

EDIE is sitting, unable to see STEPHEN, who is standing in the doorway. She sings 'Only Girl In The World'. KATE enters, singing at the top of her voice, a plate of cake in each hand. Sees STEPHEN and stops.

KATE: Oh.

STEPHEN: That's a truly horrible noise Mum.

EDIE: Who's there?

STEPHEN: Me, idiot.

KATE: Stephen.

EDIE: Who's there?

STEPHEN: The bloke you shag on Wednesdays.

EDIE: Oh you.

KATE: It's good for her.

STEPHEN: Why?

KATE: She likes it.

EDIE: It's nice.

KATE: She remembers the words.

STEPHEN: I just wish you had better taste.

EDIE: I've got wonderful taste!

KATE: What do you like anyway? Old man music I reckon.

STEPHEN: Depeche Mode are brilliant. I bet you listen to the folk revival and pretend you enjoy it.

KATE: Cake?

KATE leaves.

STEPHEN: Lovely. God I'm stiff from the car.

EDIE: What are you doing?

STEPHEN: Stretches. Chiro said it's good for me. Don't look, I get embarrassed.

EDIE: So you should. What are you doing here anyway?

STEPHEN: I had a meeting in glamorous Swindon, I thought I'd take a detour on the way back and see you.

EDIE: Ooh aren't we lucky?

KATE: Do you often have meetings in Swindon?

STEPHEN: Meetings are all people in Swindon have.

KATE: Really?

STEPHEN: It's just office after office after office, yeah. It's the life insurance capital of the world.

EDIE: Really?

STEPHEN: No, that's probably Zurich. But Swindon's like a close third, it's the big thing there. That and prostitution.

KATE: Seriously?

STEPHEN: Sort of goes with the meetings. There's a lot of trade from the company cars. They line up on the commercial roads like welcome parties.

EDIE: How distasteful.

STEPHEN: Swindon is like the Vietnam of the insurance industry. No one wants to go, but you have to go because that's where everything's happening. Then once you get there there are millions of prostitutes. But we have Paolo Di Canio running the football club instead of Robin Williams running the radio station. Which is basically the same thing.

STEPHEN exits.

EDIE: What's he doing?

STEPHEN: Sorry?

EDIE: What's he want, why's he come here?

KATE: He was just dropping by to see you.

EDIE: Don't fall for that, I know him, he wants something. Turning up like that.

KATE: Edie –

EDIE: I bet you've come to take me, has he come to take me? I don't want to go into a home. I won't know where I am.

Enter STEPHEN.

KATE: I'm sure it's nothing like that. Be calm. It's fine.

EDIE: So you just thought you'd drop by?

STEPHEN: Yeah. That OK?

EDIE: It's lovely. You've never done it before.

STEPHEN: I have.

EDIE: When?

STEPHEN: I don't know, but in the last, twenty years I will have dropped by.

EDIE: Will you.

STEPHEN: I didn't have any more meetings. I thought you'd be pleased to see me.

EDIE: Yes.

STEPHEN: But you're not.

EDIE: No, just surprised is all.

KATE: What is it you do, exactly? You're a sort of salesman, I guess? Not in a bad way, I just mean –

STEPHEN: Well –

KATE: More than the money side, / anyway.

EDIE: Terrible / at maths.

STEPHEN: Yeah. I'm in the human side.

KATE: Do you have to spend a lot of time talking to – dying people?

EDIE: Only when he comes here.

KATE: Edie.

STEPHEN: Those calls happen lower down. I manage the people who make them. Sometimes I get involved in difficult cases.

KATE: What's a difficult case in life insurance?

STEPHEN: Well, I guess – *(He nods to EDIE, who has started to hum very quietly.)*

KATE: You what?

STEPHEN: Sometimes people are insured. And they have a type of cover which might pay out if they get a certain type of illness. Like, cancer. But the guidelines on dementia make for problem cases. In a way, in a technical, legal way, someone with dementia's already dead –

KATE: Whoa –

STEPHEN: No, because it's got you, and it's going to get you completely. It's just about timing. So if I was – if you were related to someone in that situation, you could go to your insurers and say, look, if I go NHS for her care, by the time someone comes free to visit her every now and then and check she's watering her flowers she's going to be on life support. So will you pay out now so I can make her comfortable? And that would be a problem case.

KATE: Why?

STEPHEN: Because right now you can't call this a terminal illness, can you. So if I were making the judgement I wouldn't pay out. She hasn't crossed the line yet, she hasn't started actually dying, she's just old.

EDIE: You've forgotten to pretend you're not talking about me.

STEPHEN: Oh, Mum, I'm –

EDIE: It's all right. It's the council that's the pirate.

KATE: Why?

EDIE: Two years maybe before they can help you. Or you can accelerate the process if you try to kill yourself a certain number of times.

KATE: Seriously?

EDIE: I wouldn't. I used to say when I start to go gaga get the gun and shoot me, but when push comes to shove you want to stick around as long as you can.

KATE: Of course.

STEPHEN: I put Mum on a waiting list before you came. But we don't know how long it'll be.

EDIE: I wouldn't need it either.

STEPHEN: You would, it'd be someone doing everything Kate's doing and she does enough, doesn't she?

EDIE: We have Kate.

STEPHEN: I didn't know that when I put your name down, did I! Sorry. Being here sets my teeth on edge.

EDIE: Well I'm sorry for that.

STEPHEN: No, I – forget it. Where's Dad?

EDIE: Out in the fields.

STEPHEN: Course.

EDIE: He'll be hours yet. He'd be hopeless if I went into care, you know that Stephen don't you? You'd have to move in here.

STEPHEN: I couldn't, Mum.

EDIE: He wouldn't cope. You'd have to sell the farm and put him in with me. I get so scared when I think of leaving him alone and he never learned to do anything round the house.

STEPHEN: He'll be all right. He'll live twenty years to spite me.

EDIE: He's not trying to spite you! He's just no good at talking. Neither are you.

KATE: So – how are Emily and Hannah and Sam?

STEPHEN: Erm, fine, yeah. I've been travelling too much. Haven't seen enough of them. Half the time in London.

EDIE: London.

STEPHEN: It's not all bad.

EDIE: You can't fool me, I've seen how much those paninis cost.

STEPHEN: Emily thinks I crack jokes all the time to try and be like you.

EDIE: Does she? I suppose she's just trying to make you feel bad.

STEPHEN: You what?

EDIE: She always does, takes the fun out of everything.

STEPHEN: Jesus, Mum.

EDIE: Well I don't know why someone who tells a joke should have to be subjected to psychological analysis afterwards.

STEPHEN: My jokes are shit Mum, she can't exactly laugh at them, she has to say something.

EDIE: No, that's true, you don't tell the sort of jokes that are actually funny.

STEPHEN: Just the sort of jokes that make me look desperate to impress people and hopelessly insecure.

KATE: Do you think that?

STEPHEN: No, that was a joke, I think – well actually I think I fish for sympathy. Look, I'm doing it now, it's working, you're feeling sorry for me. People feel sorry for people who tell shit jokes.

KATE: Why do you want sympathy?

STEPHEN: I don't quite mean – I mean I want people to like me.

EDIE: He's always been insecure. Never had proper friends at school, never brought anyone home. Not a socialiser. When he was in junior school he told us some of the boys in his class were bullying him. We asked him what was happening. He said at breaktimes he'd walk around this white line telling himself a story, this painted line on the field above the classrooms. And at each end of the field these boys would shout at him. We asked him, when they shout at you, are you walking past some posts with a net hanging off them? And he said yes. So we told him you're walking round a football pitch, they're shouting at you because you're in front of the goal. Never been good with people, have you? Off in your own world.

STEPHEN: Thanks for that. I wish you'd go senile faster.

EDIE: That's cos you don't know about all the gambling debts you're going to inherit.

STEPHEN: Ho ho ho.

KATE: You should see someone if you feel like that about yourself.

STEPHEN: What, therapy?

KATE: I got therapy. I thought it was brilliant.

STEPHEN: Oh –

KATE: What?

STEPHEN: Well, you aside, right? But I just think, come off it. I'm living one of the best lives anyone's ever lived. I've got clean running water, my BCG, a job and kids and all my limbs, I don't need –

EDIE: Do you think you're being a bit close-minded?

STEPHEN: Therapy's for people who've been trained to think they're important by watching too much TV.

KATE: If it helps, it helps, is all –

STEPHEN: That's what fat people say when they allow themselves a biscuit.

KATE: Right.

STEPHEN: Sorry. Don't you think?

KATE: I don't know.

EDIE: I think you do.

KATE: No, actually you're right Edie, I do, of course our lives are lucky next to other people's. But the way you feel isn't relative to how other people feel, is it, it's about how you feel. It's not your fault if you're living small and your problems look trivial. That's actually half the problem.

STEPHEN: Right. Sorry.

KATE: There's nothing to apologise for.

STEPHEN: No but I am, I'm sorry.

EDIE: That's Emily as well, he apologises for everything, never used to do that.

STEPHEN: Mum.

EDIE: Well it's true, isn't it?

STEPHEN: I don't know, Mum. Let's just agree with what you think. But there are a lot of things I never used to do when I lived here. I never used to have anyone to talk to. I never used to feel able to do what I wanted and get the bus into town.

EDIE: I would have liked for you to have had someone to play with as much as you.

STEPHEN: I'm sorry, I'm snapping. We're bickerers in this family. Emily and me haven't had the chance to actually, properly, see each other in too long, so it's just a bit of a sore –

EDIE: Oh.

STEPHEN: No, it's nothing, it's just you talking about her when I feel a bit –

EDIE: Oh.

STEPHEN: Emily's good for me, you see. She sees through all – this. Chatter chatter chatter. Punctures the bubble, that's good for me. But I get back late, she gets back late, we're already asleep when the other one gets home, or whatever – you can miss people even when they're around, you know. It's all fine, Mum, it's just a bit – you know.

EDIE: Sorry.

STEPHEN: No, no.

EDIE: I do think you're unhappy though.

KATE: I had a boyfriend once was never there even when he was with me. He wanted to be a poet. He was always thinking somewhere else. It was torture really. He was in the room but then he wasn't at the same time.

EDIE: We're not our bodies, are we, we're just in them.

STEPHEN: Excuse me?

EDIE: We're not our lives either. We're just in them. We bob about and bump into each other and our lives and our bodies slip past us.

STEPHEN: You all right Mum?

EDIE: Do you feel you're off-target? I do. Bogged down in all this – living. I don't know what I was aiming for, I know I missed it. I didn't get one thing right. Crosswords, nothing that mattered.

STEPHEN: That's not true.

EDIE: No?

STEPHEN: It's not.

EDIE: All falls away though, doesn't it. Tide goes out on us. I'm sorry I'm prattling, I get so depressed. But when I say it out loud, I mean, it's important to me, it's my life, it's the most important thing in the world to me, but it's so mundane. I'm acting like it might matter to someone. And yet I feel I'm underwater.

STEPHEN: Do you need a rest, or –

KATE sings 'Mercedes Benz'. EDIE joins in.

STEPHEN: Sorry I was stressing you out.

EDIE: No, I manage that all by myself, you're all right.

KATE: Cup of tea?

EDIE: That'd be lovely.

KATE: D'you want one?

STEPHEN: Thanks.

KATE: Where's your –

STEPHEN: Oh, here. Kate?

KATE: Yeah?

STEPHEN: I was thinking we should go for a drink some time. I meant to say that, while I remember, erm. We should go for a drink, get you out of the house, sort of thing.

KATE: Oh. OK.

STEPHEN: If you fancy it.

KATE: Yeah, that'd be great. Yeah.

STEPHEN: Maybe next weekend or –

KATE: OK.

STEPHEN: Great.

KATE: I'll just get the –

Exit KATE.

EDIE: I hope that was a sensible thing you just did.

STEPHEN: Sorry?

EDIE: You know very well.

STEPHEN: I –

EDIE: It's all right, leave it.

STEPHEN: I really don't know what you mean.

EDIE: People are like glass. You see through them, you never get to them.

STEPHEN: What do you mean?

EDIE: I mean because I'm your mother I've always been able to see what you were thinking. But I don't think I've ever got you to talk to me about it once.

STEPHEN: We talk.

EDIE: There's talking and talking. The worst thing about all this is having to give up on projects I haven't even started getting to grips with.

STEPHEN: Meaning –

EDIE: I mean what if I die and I still haven't managed to have even one conversation with you.

Enter KATE.

KATE: Kettle's on.

EDIE: Who's she?

STEPHEN: Mum.

EDIE: Stephen, who's this, your friend?

KATE: Edie, it's me, it's Kate.

STEPHEN: Mum are you joking?

EDIE: She's a bit young for you Steve.

KATE: I don't think she can –

EDIE: Sorry, have we met before?

KATE: I think she's forgotten me.

EDIE: We've met before.

KATE: Yes.

EDIE: Oh. Oh yes. Sorry. I remember.

SCENE TWO

EDIE and ARTHUR are sitting in chairs, STEPHEN is standing. ARTHUR has a bit of a tractor on his lap.

STEPHEN: Funny driving through town on the way up, I recognised almost everyone.

ARTHUR: Pat Owen had a story, did you know Pat? Went away when he was young, farmed elsewhere and never

59

came home for forty years. When he did come back, twenty years ago now maybe, he got off the bus feeling the whole world was going to stop for him, like something real was happening, and an old boy sitting on the fence looked up and said hello Pat, haven't seen you in a while. And that was it. I imagine he took a draw on his pipe. Faces never change here. Except yours. So what do you want to talk about?

STEPHEN: Well –

ARTHUR: Can you help? It's a fiddle.

STEPHEN: Sure, what do I –

ARTHUR: Just sort of – I need you to hold this flush – OK?

STEPHEN: Yep.

ARTHUR: Right.

STEPHEN: Is your lap the best place, or –

ARTHUR: We could do it on the floor?

STEPHEN: Shall we do that?

ARTHUR: Yep.

STEPHEN: There you go.

ARTHUR: So the thing is it won't be level if you let it touch the floor, you have to hold it up so it's like, proud like –

STEPHEN: Got it.

EDIE: Can I help?

ARTHUR: You're all right. Right. So what do you want to talk about?

STEPHEN: Well, I was talking to Kate last week, did you know I popped in last week?

ARTHUR: Oh yeah.

STEPHEN: We were talking about – insurance. Because I'm a fascinating conversationalist, and we kind of revisited something you and I have talked about before, but things I hadn't thought about in a little –

ARTHUR: Careful.

STEPHEN: What?

ARTHUR: It's not –

STEPHEN: It'll be all right when it tightens.

ARTHUR: Not if you hold it like that.

STEPHEN: OK, so what –

ARTHUR: A bit more – yep. That'll do it. Go on.

STEPHEN: Well we were talking about early payouts. Do you remember we talked about that before?

ARTHUR: Oh yeah.

STEPHEN: And I was telling her how difficult it was to get one, but while I was driving home I got to thinking about Mum's –

ARTHUR: Hopeless.

STEPHEN: What?

ARTHUR: See. I've done too many, my hand's too tired.

STEPHEN: Why don't you hold and I'll screw? As the bishop said to the actress.

ARTHUR: What?

STEPHEN: Nothing. Why don't we swap?

ARTHUR: Do you think you could get it in properly?

STEPHEN: There you go again.

ARTHUR: What?

STEPHEN: Nothing.

EDIE: Are you fighting?

ARTHUR: No. Can you do it?

STEPHEN: I'll have a go.

ARTHUR: Come round here and I'll go round there.

STEPHEN: OK. This one?

ARTHUR: Yep.

STEPHEN: So I went back to – Mum's documents, basically, when I got home. And the thing is, I got her a pretty good – policy. How's that?

ARTHUR: Bit more.

STEPHEN: And I reckon I could get some money now if I set my mind to it. You know, get her properly looked after.

ARTHUR: Oh.

STEPHEN: So I thought I'd talk to you.

ARTHUR: Right.

STEPHEN: How's that?

ARTHUR: That's it.

He gets up and picks up the part.

STEPHEN: Where are you going?

ARTHUR: I'll just put it back on while there's some –

STEPHEN: Right.

ARTHUR: OK?

STEPHEN: I just thought we were talking about –

ARTHUR: Yeah. I'll just do this then we can talk.

STEPHEN: OK.

Exit ARTHUR.

STEPHEN: You all right Mum?

EDIE: Tired.

STEPHEN: Oh yeah. Where's Kate?

EDIE: Out.

STEPHEN: Do you want a drink, or –

EDIE: No.

STEPHEN: Have you had an OK day?

EDIE: No. I need –

STEPHEN: What?

EDIE: I need, erm – *(She gestures to her chair.)*

STEPHEN: What do you mean, Mum, are you uncomfortable?

EDIE: Yeah.

STEPHEN: OK. Let's move you a bit then, would that help? Come on.

EDIE: Yeah.

STEPHEN: You're sitting on – you're sitting on all carrier bags.

EDIE: Yeah.

STEPHEN: What are you doing that for? Course you're uncomfortable, you're all –

Enter ARTHUR.

ARTHUR: It's no good, my eyes, we left it too late. I'll have to do it in the morning.

STEPHEN: Why's Mum sitting on all these carrier bags?

ARTHUR: In case she forgets to go to the toilet.

STEPHEN: Does that happen?

ARTHUR: Just a couple of times. And I'm out all day and Kate had to go to do the shopping, so –

STEPHEN: But she's started –

ARTHUR: A bit.

STEPHEN: Oh –

EDIE: Sorry.

STEPHEN: No, no, Mum –

ARTHUR: She's all right while Kate's here.

STEPHEN: Yeah. But we need to make a plan, Dad, she's getting worse so fast.

ARTHUR: She's fine.

STEPHEN: But she's –

ARTHUR: I know. I know.

STEPHEN: Strange how men get shy when they don't want to talk.

ARTHUR: Strange how men never want to talk to each other.

STEPHEN: Shall we sit down?

ARTHUR: OK.

They sit.

STEPHEN: So I think I could get some money for care.

EDIE: What?

STEPHEN: Don't worry, Mum.

ARTHUR: Could she be looked after here?

STEPHEN: Maybe.

ARTHUR: Just –

STEPHEN: It depends what she needs, they'd make an assessment.

ARTHUR: So you'd just move her –

STEPHEN: No, Dad, I'm just trying to be realistic. Some time soon, I'm really sorry but the way things are going some time soon –

ARTHUR: Could I go with her?

STEPHEN: Maybe. Some places do that. Do you want to?

ARTHUR: I don't want her to go. I don't want to sell the farm.

STEPHEN: We maybe wouldn't need to sell the farm if I got –

ARTHUR: But there's no point havin it if she's not here. You wouldn't want it.

STEPHEN: No, but you could come back when –

ARTHUR: I couldn't. I couldn't.

STEPHEN: The other thing is, Dad, it might not be possible for you to go with her. We'll need to be ready for that. Some places do it but not everywhere, OK?

ARTHUR: I'd rather put it off as late as we can then.

STEPHEN: What do you mean?

ARTHUR: I'd rather she was here until she absolutely couldn't be.

STEPHEN: Even if that wasn't the best for Mum?

ARTHUR: What d'you mean, it's her home, it's our life, of course it's best for her!

EDIE: Sssh, boys.

ARTHUR: Sorry love. Of course it's best.

STEPHEN: Even if a nurse said –

ARTHUR: I'm pretty sure she's going to keep wanting to be here till she absolutely can't be, all right? That's all.

STEPHEN: OK. I think I probably need to make you aware of something else too. Not a – just something that might be relevant. Erm, Emily and me are having trouble. And she's kind of said to me, kind of that she's not sure we should be together. Or married. And we're kind of talking about me moving out, because we – fight, and it upsets the kids, and they have exams, you know?

ARTHUR: Right.

STEPHEN: And I'm just telling you this because it might mean my life's about to change quite a lot. And I'm not sure how, but right now I'm visiting a lot, and I don't know – and it's on my mind that Kate might not be here for ever, and if she leaves and I can't help and you're having to put down carrier bags already –

EDIE: It was my idea the bags. I told him to get them.

STEPHEN: Oh yeah?

EDIE: Good idea.

STEPHEN: Absolutely, yeah.

ARTHUR: I'm sorry about you and Emily, Steve.

STEPHEN: Oh. Thanks.

ARTHUR: I mean, yeah. Do you think it's a passing thing, or –

STEPHEN: I don't know really.

ARTHUR: How are you feeling about it?

STEPHEN: Erm. Underwater.

ARTHUR: Right. I can see what you're saying. I can see it affects – we do know you come here as much as you can, we do appreciate it.

STEPHEN: Well –

ARTHUR: If it helps, she's never been good enough for you. I've never liked her. I mean, it might not be the worst thing that happened, you know?

STEPHEN: Right.

ARTHUR: Is that the wrong thing –

STEPHEN: She's the mother of my children and I've been married to her for almost twenty years.

ARTHUR: Right. Sorry. Yeah.

STEPHEN: Can we get back to –

ARTHUR: Yeah. So you want to –

STEPHEN: Look into getting the insurance money.

ARTHUR: I guess that makes –

STEPHEN: Yeah?

ARTHUR: Do we need to start thinking about selling the farm?

STEPHEN: Do you want to?

ARTHUR: I don't want to be here once she's not.

STEPHEN: Are you sure? You love it here.

ARTHUR: No. Only the people living on it. Only the life here, not the place. I'd go.

STEPHEN: Would you?

ARTHUR: It's too – it'd be too –

STEPHEN: Yeah.

EDIE: You wouldn't sell it would you?

ARTHUR: Don't worry love, we're talking hypothetically.

EDIE: Did they go bust or have enough, the Joneses, which was it? Or did they just get old?

STEPHEN: What if we met an estate agent then?

ARTHUR: I know what he'd say.

STEPHEN: What?

ARTHUR: That no one'll want it. Farming like it is, housing like it is, no one'll want this. I'm under no illusions about what I've got here.

STEPHEN: Don't feel sorry for yourself.

ARTHUR: I'm sorry, but it's hard not to. You look at a wheat field all your life. It's a beautiful view, how it changes as the year rolls round. But at the same time it's not much of the world, is it. Now I'm getting left here. I just wish it was me it happened to.

STEPHEN: Yeah. Yeah, me too.

SCENE THREE

EDIE is alone on stage.

EDIE: Ever watch the light cross this wall? Outline of the window crossing that stone, that's the whole earth spinning, whole lives changing. You can watch it all from here. In my dream he comes to me and we say all these things we've never said to each other before. And he's happy.

Enter STEPHEN.

STEPHEN: You on your own?

EDIE: You're all dressed up.

STEPHEN: Erm –

EDIE: Smart.

STEPHEN: Yeah. Is Kate –

EDIE: What?

STEPHEN: Upstairs?

EDIE: I don't know. Are you all dressed up for her?

STEPHEN: No.

EDIE: Are you?

STEPHEN: No.

EDIE: Why?

STEPHEN: Mum, I'm not dressed up, don't worry about it.

EDIE: Have you got a date? You never had a date.

STEPHEN: Mum –

Enter KATE.

KATE: All right?

STEPHEN: Fine thanks. You?

KATE: Yeah.

STEPHEN: Great. Still on for tonight?

KATE: I can't, I'm sorry.

STEPHEN: Oh.

KATE: I can't go out tonight.

STEPHEN: Oh. OK.

KATE: I think you might have said something before I came home and found a for sale sign on the driveway.

STEPHEN: What?

EDIE: What are you selling?

KATE: I'm not saying it's anything to do with – but I am living here, you might have said.

STEPHEN: About selling the house?

KATE: Yeah. I didn't know I needed to be making other plans. I do now. But –

STEPHEN: It's going to be ages, we'll never sell it, that's a formality, just –

KATE: Right.

STEPHEN: Is that why you can't come out? I'm sorry, I didn't think, I didn't realise. You were out when me and Dad planned it and then I've been doing it all in Salisbury, I haven't seen you.

KATE: I just got here as well.

STEPHEN: I'm sorry. I didn't think –

KATE: I know it's nothing to do with me. But I just got here. It's like getting chucked.

STEPHEN: No –

KATE: Everyone I ever have anything to do with ends up doing this. It's just so boring, people not thinking of you. I'll have to go.

STEPHEN: No.

KATE: Well I'll have to make plans and I'll have to go when something comes up. I can't hang around here till you kick me out.

STEPHEN: It was never a permanent –

KATE: No, I know. But notice, that's all I want. A bit of warning. So I feel like you thought of me. Which you didn't. I'm sorry. I'm getting so angry, I'm so rude.

STEPHEN: Don't –

KATE: And you're putting your fucking Mum in a home! I don't work so you'll put her in a home.

STEPHEN: Right.

KATE: I'm not saying I feel, I know I was a temporary – but look at her, she's still – how can you do that?

STEPHEN: She's not always going to be –

KATE: No, but how can you just shovel her off like that? And turfing your Dad out of here, how can you do that? And then fucking asking me out in front of your Mum, when you're married, when you have kids my age, and turning up like this? You don't give a fuck about anything.

STEPHEN: I didn't –

KATE: No?

STEPHEN: What?

KATE: Say what you were going to say. You didn't ask me out? You're holding a bunch of flowers.

STEPHEN: They're –

KATE: You've never bought her flowers, there are never flowers in the house.

STEPHEN: Right.

KATE: Look, I'm sorry, I'm being so rude. You're a nice man, you are, and you've sorted me out a bit. But you don't think about anything. I mean how dare you? How can you bump me around like this, sell the house I'm staying in and not think to tell me, then turn up hoping for – what? A snog in your car after you've had too many?

STEPHEN: That's why you're angry.

KATE: All of that is why I'm angry. Because you brought flowers. Because you're having her carted off. Because your Dad wanders round looking lost and frowning at the sign on the drive. Because you're pulling the rug out from under my feet and it's not even important enough for you to notice you're doing it. You're every fucking man I've ever dated.

STEPHEN: I just saw these, I thought they were nice.

KATE: Hopeless. Look, I know I'm being rude talking like this, I know, I will go, I know this is out of order. But you need to hear it man.

STEPHEN: You don't –

KATE: Yeah, I do have to go.

STEPHEN: It's a formality, it's a fucking – so I bought these, yeah. I thought I would, I thought it was a bit bold but I thought I would. Because my wife's filed for a divorce because she's – bored of me, I don't know, and I thought I'd cheer myself up. And that sounds like I'm using you but it doesn't feel like that, I just think you're fun. You're funny. You're beautiful. And I wanted to spend some time with you, and – be around you. I look at you, I think if I could take it all back, do it again, try something different, I would. In a heartbeat. You've still got it in front of you and that's amazing. What have I got? Kids I'll see at weekends. Unfulfilled potential. They have each other. You have the future. So I bought you flowers. And I'm sorry I didn't tell you about Mum or the house, but the thing is, I don't mean to be cruel, but it's nothing really to do with you. You're a visitor here. This is family. It's a family thing.

KATE: It's hard to feel like everything's in front of you if the whole world's just men dropping you when it suits them.

STEPHEN: That's not what's happening. Look, won't you come for a drink? We could talk this over?

KATE: I'm sorry, I can't be bothered, Stephen. I just can't be arsed.

STEPHEN: So what? You're ordering me out of my house?

EDIE: It's not.

STEPHEN: What?

EDIE: You walked out long ago.

Enter ARTHUR.

ARTHUR: Evening all. Hello Steve, you all right?

STEPHEN: Hi.

ARTHUR: Staying for supper?

EDIE: He can't, love.

ARTHUR: Just dropping by? How was your day, love?

EDIE: All right.

ARTHUR: Wouldn't put the kettle on would you Steve? I'm parched.

STEPHEN: I'm sorry, I can't, I've got to go.

ARTHUR: Already?

STEPHEN: I'm sorry. I've got to go.

Exit STEPHEN.

ARTHUR: What was the matter with him?

EDIE: Oh, no. Oh, no no no.

KATE: Are you all right?

EDIE gets up.

EDIE: I don't feel well.

ARTHUR: Is she all right?

EDIE: I remembered the letters.

KATE: What letters Edie?

EDIE: Yesterday, yesterday, didn't I.

KATE: What?

EDIE: I remembered them look.

She picks up a pile of opened letters.

EDIE: They're trying to send me a credit card. They're trying to sell me catalogue. I ought to reply.

ARTHUR: Oh yes.

EDIE: But I had to hide them because I felt so sad.

ARTHUR: What about?

EDIE: Well –

KATE: What made you sad?

EDIE: I just don't think I'll ever go on another holiday.

SCENE FOUR

EDIE, ARTHUR and KATE.

EDIE: Is it today that you're leaving?

KATE: After you've had your lunch.

EDIE: Is Stephen coming to look after us like you?

KATE: Not like –

EDIE: Oh yes. And why have you got so many boxes?

KATE: These aren't for me, these are your things.

EDIE: Why are my things all in boxes?

ARTHUR: It's all right Edie, don't worry.

EDIE: Are we going away? Is it a holiday?

ARTHUR: No, it's not a holiday. Don't you remember I said?

EDIE: What?

ARTHUR: What?

EDIE: Said what?

ARTHUR: Don't you remember I told you what was happening?

EDIE: I give up.

ARTHUR: It's all right, don't worry.

EDIE: It isn't a holiday? That's a shame.

KATE: Can I get you both a cup of tea?

ARTHUR: That would be lovely.

KATE: OK.

Exit KATE.

EDIE: I thought you were unfaithful to me one time.

ARTHUR: Say what?

EDIE: I went into town, not long after we were married, and you were sitting in the window of a hotel with a woman having lunch. I didn't know what to think. I never brought it up, I just came home.

ARTHUR: You didn't think –

EDIE: Not really, no. I've always known you were a good boy. That is your redeeming feature.

ARTHUR: That's what makes me so bloody dull.

EDIE: Yes, you're a straight and narrow road, you.

ARTHUR: What?

EDIE: A straight and narrow road.

ARTHUR: I'm what, Streatham what?

EDIE: A straight and narrow road!

ARTHUR: Oh!

EDIE: Silly.

ARTHUR: My ears.

EDIE: You do make me laugh.

ARTHUR: I don't even remember it. I don't know when you'd be talking about. Sometimes buyers used to meet me with their wives –

EDIE: It's all right. I knew you were a good boy really. I'm only sorry I never asked, it makes it look like I wouldn't have believed you. Perhaps I wouldn't have, I don't know. I believe you now. It's sad, isn't it. Her and Stephen.

ARTHUR: What?

EDIE: Oh, Arthur, really?

ARTHUR: What about her and Stephen?

EDIE: Oh, you are odd. If I felt a bit stronger today I would tell him what he should be doing is leaving his wife. Wouldn't that end up better for both of them? She can't be happy either. Not that I know.

ARTHUR: Actually, they're –

EDIE: What?

ARTHUR: No, no.

EDIE: What?

ARTHUR: No, forget it.

EDIE: I probably will.

ARTHUR: I don't know what the point of me would have been if you'd ever left me.

EDIE: No, but we were lucky. We didn't have to think about things like that.

Enter KATE.

EDIE: Are you all right about going away?

KATE: Me?

EDIE: Are you all right about things?

KATE: Well. Yeah, I'm fine. I mean I'm sad, but I'm fine. I'm going to go and look for something else now.

ARTHUR: Do you know what yet?

KATE: No.

ARTHUR: Word of advice?

KATE: Yeah?

ARTHUR: We're in between everything. Nothing ever happens, you shouldn't go looking for that. You'll never stop wanting. The trick is to steer between everything.

EDIE: All you have to do really is get through it all OK and get through to your grave without too much trouble.

KATE: Right. Yeah. I suppose.

EDIE: We were going to have three or four children. One to take over from us and one we thought might teach and we hoped to have a student. We thought we might have a child went into the church, we could have got behind that. But the appetite had gone out of us to be all supporting someone's – what's his name? My son, his name is Stephen. And it was sort of lovely when he married because of course you can live it all again with grandchildren, but it's not the same. Or it wasn't for us. We weren't quite allowed to be involved. You're practically the same age as his children, I don't know what he was thinking, I don't know how he can be so unhappy. I don't know what makes you so unhappy either. I just don't know why you have so many boxes.

ARTHUR: Edie –

Enter STEPHEN.

STEPHEN: Sorry I'm late.

KATE: You OK?

STEPHEN: Yeah. OK. Bad morning.

ARTHUR: We were starting to wonder whether you'd got lost.

STEPHEN: I've come here enough Dad, I wouldn't get lost. You've already done so much packing.

ARTHUR: Up all night.

STEPHEN: I've cleared the whole day –

ARTHUR: It's finished. We can spend the day moving it, can't we.

STEPHEN: Yeah, fine. You look tired.

ARTHUR: Your mother's tired as well.

STEPHEN: Hi Mum, sorry. You OK?

EDIE: I feel quite tired.

KATE: Do you want lunch before I go?

STEPHEN: Are you leaving already?

KATE: I've got to get a train.

STEPHEN: There are trains all day, aren't there?

KATE: I've got to get this one.

ARTHUR: There's the fish pie you cooked for yesterday's dinner, we could have that for lunch?

EDIE: That sounds nice.

KATE: Shall I heat it up?

ARTHUR: Thank you, love.

KATE: I'll be a minute.

Exit KATE.

ARTHUR: OK?

STEPHEN: Yeah, just –

ARTHUR: What's up?

STEPHEN: What do I have to do for you to stop talking to me like that? What have I done that offends you so much?

ARTHUR: What are you / talking –

STEPHEN: You think I'm hopeless.

ARTHUR: No –

STEPHEN: You do, I know you do. It's you two make me a failure. Sitting there together like that, happy like that, what kind of pressure do you think that puts on me?

ARTHUR: Well –

STEPHEN: You look at me like I'm wasting my life. You act like my whole life is a way of trying to disappoint you.

Enter KATE.

KATE: We OK?

STEPHEN: Fine.

KATE: Do you want feeding?

STEPHEN: Are we feeding her now?

EDIE: Yes please.

STEPHEN: Are we feeding –

ARTHUR: I'll do it.

KATE: You sure?

STEPHEN: I didn't know about this.

ARTHUR: Give it here. There we go love.

EDIE: Thank you. I'm sorry.

ARTHUR: I'm sorry too love. There we go. All right.

EDIE: Is this the last meal we'll eat in our house?

ARTHUR: Yes, it is.

EDIE: It seems such a long time we've spent here. But it's not a long time really.

A car beeps.

KATE: That's me. I called a cab.

STEPHEN: I could have given you a lift.

KATE: I didn't want to be any trouble.

STEPHEN: I would have liked to have given you a lift.

KATE: You don't get to try and be friends with me, Stephen. Don't you understand that?

STEPHEN: I was thinking while we drove over the Plain, what would it be like if we did what we wanted, you know? What would happen if I walked out of here, I don't know, if I walked out of here now and left with you?

KATE: That's not what you want.

STEPHEN: No –

KATE: You just don't want to be who you are. I don't know if this occurred to you as being relevant, but it's not what I want either.

ARTHUR: Steve?

STEPHEN: Dad?

ARTHUR: Will you help me up? She's done. My knees.

STEPHEN: Sure. There you go. That's all right.

KATE: Do you want your lunch now Arthur?

Beep.

ARTHUR: Yes please.

KATE: I have to go.

EDIE: Kate?

KATE: Yes?

EDIE: You are very beautiful my love. You bear that in mind, all right? For as long as you're young and can enjoy it you should know that's what's happening to you.

ARTHUR: It's been such a help you being here.

KATE: I'm so sorry that –

Beep.

STEPHEN: Kate.

KATE: Yeah?

STEPHEN: I don't know. Keep in touch?

EDIE: I don't think so, dear.

Exit KATE.

ARTHUR: Can I have my lunch?

STEPHEN: Yeah.

ARTHUR: Then you and I can start packing the car.

STEPHEN: Yeah.

ARTHUR: Any news from the estate agent?

STEPHEN: No, sorry. You ever read any of these?

ARTHUR: They're your mother's. Do you read much?

STEPHEN: A bit.

EDIE: I collected them by subscription.

STEPHEN: Yeah?

EDIE: Bookcase came the same way. Subscription, and they sent a book a month. And a bookcase when you paid your first money, that you one day filled. News from the big world.

STEPHEN: That's a lovely idea.

EDIE: Must be sets like that all over England. Little escapes, little trapdoors out.

ARTHUR: I'd rather go for a walk.

STEPHEN: Did you ever read Trollope?

ARTHUR: No.

STEPHEN: I hated Trollope.

ARTHUR: The Scottish one?

STEPHEN: No, that's Walter Scott. I need to ask you something.

ARTHUR: Oh yeah?

STEPHEN: I was wondering whether it might be helpful if I came and stayed here for a bit. For the first few weeks. Or just while we get it sold, you know? Help you keep it ticking over.

ARTHUR: Joking?

STEPHEN: Why –

ARTHUR: We'll come to blows, Steve, you know we will, are you joking? Why would you want to do that?

STEPHEN: No –

ARTHUR: It's kind of you to think of me but really –

STEPHEN: Actually –

ARTHUR: I know how you feel about this. Me. I don't mind. Or I've come to terms, anyway, heh! I'll be all right, yeah? You just get this place sold and get me somewhere near her.

STEPHEN: Actually Dad Emily's kind of kicked me out of the house. So I was wondering whether I could stay here just while I haven't got anywhere else to go.

ARTHUR: Oh. Right. I see.

STEPHEN: But obviously I did think it would be good, now you're going to be – but maybe while I'm getting it sold I could just sort myself out too, you know?

ARTHUR: Of course. You're always welcome here, Steve, always have been.

EDIE: It's your home.

STEPHEN: Yeah.

EDIE: It's our home.

ARTHUR: All right Edie love. So you'll stay for a bit.

STEPHEN: Thank you.

ARTHUR: OK.

EDIE: Is it nice this place I'm going to?

STEPHEN: Yeah. It's nice.

EDIE: People always used to say we lived out the back of beyond. Will you come and visit me, d'you think?

STEPHEN: As often as I can.

EDIE: And you'll visit me, won't you, Arthur? And look after the house? And remember to change the sheets? And kill the chickens when you move away, don't leave them alone will you? And keep the machines in good nick? What will I do while you're packing?

ARTHUR: *(Goes to her.)* It's all right, my love. I'm going to look after you. It's going to be all right. There you go. Are you tired? It's going to be all right. Why don't you have a lie down?

EDIE: That'd be nice.

ARTHUR: Shall I help you to bed?

EDIE: Thank you. You'll be all right with him, won't you Stephen? You won't let him fall down or anything.

ARTHUR: You used to say that sort of thing to me about him.

EDIE: Yes, well it's all swings and roundabouts isn't it. Come on.

ARTHUR: There we go.

EDIE: This is the poem of my life. I cannot remember almost everything I have ever done. I cannot remember the names of the children who sat next to me at school. I can hardly tell which of the millions of lives I imagined I might have lived eventually turned out to be the real one. They are all as vivid and vague as each other. Sometimes I cry. It's not even bad yet, sometimes I can't help it. What I remember is light through trees and light on water in the morning and a woman in a white dress and the way the light through my eyelids found me when I used to sunbathe. And your shadow falling over my eyes so I opened them and looked up to see you standing there looking down. My legs in the sun. What I remember is Sundays and walking back from church and my hand in your hand. And you are in all of my dreams because you were there in my life as well.

Exit EDIE and ARTHUR.

STEPHEN looks around. He picks up a box.

END.

EVENTIDE

For Dad.

You're pretending this isn't your life. You think it's going to happen some other time. When you're dead you'll realise you were alive now.

Caryl Churchill, *Mad Forest*

Characters

MARK
20s, a regular at the White Horse

JOHN
about 50, a pub landlord

LIZ
about 40, a church organist

The play is set round the back of the White
Horse pub in Hampshire.

Eventide was first presented by Up In Arms and Arcola Theatre in association with the North Wall on September 25th, 2015, with the following company:

Hasan Dixon – MARK
James Doherty – JOHN
Ellie Piercy – LIZ

Director, Alice Hamilton
Designer, James Perkins
Lighting Designer, Simon Gethin Thomas
Sound Designer, George Dennis
Production Manager, Tamsin Rose
Company Stage Manager, Charlie Young
Assistant Stage Manager, Rebecca Denby
Costume Supervisor, Jennie Quirk
Producer, Chloe Courtney
Assistant Director, George Nichols
Marketing and Producing Assistant, Rachael Harrison

SCENE ONE

MARK is sitting with a toolkit. Enter JOHN, pushing a wheelbarrow.

JOHN: Bloke walks into a pub. And he goes to the bar and orders a pint and while he's waiting for it this feller sidles up to him and says do you wanna buy a ferret? Scuse me? Our hero replies. Do you wanna buy a ferret? The feller says again. Not really says our man. Ah, but this is no ordinary ferret, says the other feller. No no no. This ferret gives the best blow job in the world. You what? Says the first bloke. I'm telling you, says the stranger, I am in possession of a ferret that gives the best blow job in the world. However, it's coming up Christmas and I've got a tax bill to pay, so I need to realise some of my assets, and for that reason I'm willing to let you have this ferret for the ever so reasonable sum of five hundred quid. A monkey for a ferret? Asks the first bloke. Monkey's five hundred quid, Mark, in case you're not as down with the kids as I am. Case you're not street. Where was I? Tell you what, says the other feller, don't just take my word for it. I can see you're the sort of bloke likes to know what he's buying, fair enough. I respect that. I admire it. So why not pop in the gents and give him a test run? And he slips this ferret in the other feller's pocket, and the other feller's not sure what to do so rather than give it back and risk offence, he goes off to the gents. He's English, see, he doesn't want to say no directly. So he goes in this cubicle, and he's alone with this ferret, and he thinks, this has got to be a practical joke. There's no way I'm letting my cock anywhere near this ferret's teeth. But he's in the cubicle now. He'll feel like an idiot if he comes out without having tried it. And he thinks to himself, wouldn't it be amazing if it was true? Wouldn't it be an amazing thing if there was a ferret who gave the best blow job in the world? And isn't that worth a little risk, a thought like that? So he takes a deep breath, and opens his flies, and five minutes later he's back in the bar with a grin a mile wide saying he has to get to a cash point. So he buys this ferret, and takes it home, and he shows it to

his wife. I've bought a ferret, he says. Why? Says the wife.
Well this is no ordinary ferret, he says. This ferret gives
the best blow job in the world. That's wonderful, says his
wife, but what do you want me to do with it? Easy, he says.
Teach it to cook and fuck off.

MARK laughs.

MARK: That's good that is, I like that.

JOHN: Mm.

MARK: It's got a twist at the –

JOHN: Jokes don't want deconstructing, Mark, it spoils 'em.
Let it remain as a beautiful snowflake.

MARK: Right. Yeah.

JOHN starts to fill the wheelbarrow with firewood.

MARK: Stocking up?

JOHN: Mm.

MARK: Hot day for a fire.

JOHN: Blaze in my grate every day of the year. It's part of
what people come for, you know?

MARK: Oh yeah.

JOHN: Horrible mangy dogs and an unpleasantly hot public
bar. That's what I'm selling really. More than the ham
egg and chips. All kinds of places shift food and drink,
it's sweat and dogs make me distinctive. I'd be down on
couples booking dirty weekends if I didn't have a flickering
log fire to offer them, and the infidelity trade's big business.
People having affairs tip well out of guilt.

MARK: Fair enough.

JOHN: She meant a lot to you didn't she.

MARK: Not – yeah. She did, yeah.

JOHN: I suppose it's not my place.

MARK: You're all right.

JOHN: Guess you're getting it from everyone.

MARK: Not every one's got as big a mouth as you.

JOHN: That's my job, isn't it. Ask all the awkward questions.
Listen to all the awkward answers. Know all the secrets.
That's the art. Innit. Sometimes all your life feels like a
falling away of everything from you, don't you think? I
think that. And when you get to considering it, it's hard to
see the point really, innit. Where was I? You have to carry
on though.

MARK: No 'have to' about it, far as I see.

JOHN: Mm?

MARK: Time just keeps fuckin' happenin' to you, don't it.
'Have to' makes it sound like there's a – I dunno, like
there's a choice. It's more like – it's like you're on a
Megabus, right, or maybe a National Express, I dunno, and
you pass a crash on the other side of the motorway, and
you want to have a look, you know? But before you can get
a proper goosey you're past it, and the road's going on, and
you're hurried away from the scene of the accident. Like.
Yeah. Because you're headed for Plymouth or wherever,
you weren't meant to stop there. That's what absolutely
everything is like. Fuck it, anyway. How are you John, are
you all right? It's not a great day for you either is it.

JOHN: Today?

MARK: What with –

JOHN: I know what you're saying. It's not great, no.

MARK: What will you do, do you think?

JOHN: I don't know. Sit perfectly still. Don't have the energy
for anything except a drink.

MARK: It's not good, man.

JOHN: Not in the long run, no, but I get a certain bitter
pleasure from it now. And I don't know what's so wrong
with sitting perfectly still. When Chris Marsden announced
he was going to retire – you remember Chris Marsden,
used to play centre mid for Southampton? – he went on
the radio and said his plan was to go to a beach in Greece
and just sit there. In the sun. And the interviewer asked
him, joking like, don't you think you'll get bored? He just
laughed, he said no mate, I think I'll get tanned.

MARK laughs.

JOHN: You ever read W.H.Davies?

MARK: Don't think so.

JOHN: He was a tramp. And a poet. For a little while he lived
in a shed at the bottom of Edward Thomas's garden. Who
was a manic depressive. And also a poet, who died in the
war. Which is one of the best comedies never written. Not
the war, the two poets. And W.H.Davies wrote this poem,
'a poor life this if, full of care, we have no time to stand and
stare'. You know that?

MARK: *Four Weddings and a Funeral.*

JOHN: It was the Centre Parcs advert actually, but never mind.
What I'm saying is, W.H.Davies, when he was living in
Edward Thomas's shed, he wasn't a million miles from
here. All in the shadow of the Forest. Same as Chrissy
Marsden, see? And I don't think people recognise that
there's a distinctive outlook which belongs to this part of
the world, which is about sitting around doing fuck all
for as long as you possibly can. That's what it's all about
isn't it, pubs and cricket or whatever. Sitting around doing
nothing. And people associate that with laziness, but it's
not. It's the embodiment of a – of a philosophy.

MARK: What?

John: They toil not, neither do they spin.

Mark: What?

John: Bible, innit. You know that one don't you? Bible's full
of stuff about not having to work. Parable of the prodigal
son's all about that. Fucking, don't worry about putting a
shift in, fuck off on a jolly and we'll do you a roast.

Mark: Yeah, I never get that one.

John: Why?

MARK: I don't know why people give more credit to the bloke
who fucked off and cocked up then came home than the
bloke who stuck around and got on with things.

JOHN: I think it's about getting converts.

MARK: How?

JOHN: Well it was a new religion wasn't it. Christianity. So it
was like a message to say, be nice to floating voters. They'll
end up deciding the election.

MARK: Right.

JOHN: Or something else.

MARK: What?

JOHN: Well I was just thinking, maybe it's a way of saying, try
and do something with your life. Be deliberate, you know?
During your life, try and make one conscious decision. Cos
you'll always have where you came from. So you might as
well have a go at trying to find something else for as long
as you've got a home to come back to, and not just truck
along the same furrow for ever.

MARK: It'll all get better, you know, John.

JOHN: It might get number. I'll give you that. But it'll always
have happened, and nothing that's happened to you, really
happened to you like that ever gets better, does it. It might

get number, I'll give you that. Look at me. I ought to be comforting you.

MARK: No –

JOHN: You did care for her, didn't you.

MARK: It's strange. Cos I did, I can admit that now, I did. Yeah. And I feel – but I've no more right to grieve than anyone else, have I. Cos. No reason to feel any – more than anyone else. We were close for a while, at school or whatever, yeah, and I loved all that, when we were at school, but not for any real reason, only because we shared a few classes, you know? And I've never had the kind of girlfriend where you're – you know, where you're happy, so I don't know, but I think people who are close like, I mean properly close, like, maybe I mean people who are in love, sort of thing, there must always be more to it than that, mustn't there? Some – feeling you both have, which is more than just sharing a few classes, and you fancying her and her not minding you. Which is more or less. Maybe not for the likes of me, maybe I'll end up taking what I can get or have to stay on my own for ever, or whatever, but for the likes of her, you know? There must be actual love that's like a thing, that exists. So I don't feel more important than anyone else. No. I don't feel I should be, anyway. So it's strange how I'm feeling today.

JOHN: How, strange?

MARK: Because I loved her, to be honest. Yeah. Yeah. I've never said that to anyone before.

JOHN: Not even to her?

MARK: Course not. Fuck. Last of all to her.

JOHN: But you loved her.

MARK: I still do. That doesn't stop, does it.

JOHN: No. It just becomes something you can cope with. Or that's what we must both hope.

MARK: Sometimes I sort of wish I'd never felt anything in my life.

JOHN: I hear that.

MARK: Yeah?

JOHN: Look at us. Do you want a drink?

MARK: I'd better not.

JOHN: Let me stand you a beer. You're earning that today. This is my last day as a landlord, let me stand you a beer.

MARK: Just a bottle, not a pint.

JOHN: All right. I might have one with you.

MARK: Don't you need to start prepping lunch mate?

JOHN: In a bit. There's a little while left.

Enter LIZ.

LIZ: Morning!

JOHN: Hello Liz, you all right?

LIZ: I'm OK, how are you?

JOHN: Wanna hear a joke?

LIZ: Really?

JOHN: Go on, little joke.

LIZ: Go on then.

JOHN: Bloke walks into a pub. And he goes to the bar and orders a pint and while he's waiting this feller sidles up to him and says do you wanna buy a ferret? Scuse me? Our hero replies. Do you wanna buy a ferret? The feller says again. Not really. Ah, but this is no ordinary ferret, says the other feller. This ferret gives the best blow job in the world. You what? Asks the first bloke. I'm telling you, says the stranger, I am in possession of a ferret that gives the best blow job in the world. However, it's coming up for Christmas and I've got a tax bill to pay, so I'm gonna let you have it for the ever so reasonable sum of five hundred quid. Five hundred quid for a ferret? Asks the first bloke. Tell you what, says the other feller, you don't just have to take my word for it. Why not pop in the gents and give the little feller a test run? And he slips this ferret in the other feller's pocket, and the other feller goes off to the gents, and ten minutes later he's back in the bar with a grin a mile wide saying he has to get to a cash point. So he buys this ferret, and takes it home, and he shows it to his wife. I've bought a ferret, he says. Why? Says the wife. Well this is no ordinary ferret, he says. This ferret gives the best blow job in the world. That's wonderful, says his wife, but what do you want me to do with it? Easy, he says. Teach it to cook and fuck off.

MARK laughs again. LIZ doesn't.

LIZ: You're awful, John, you know that?

JOHN: It's a reputation I try to live down to. Lemonade?

LIZ: Yes please.

JOHN: I'll get it.

LIZ: You don't have to –

JOHN: Glad to. Don't worry. Always silver service when you come to The White Horse.

LIZ: Well. Thanks.

Exit JOHN with the wheelbarrow, which is now full of firewood. LIZ lights up.

LIZ: Sorry – do you mind if I smoke?

MARK: Go ahead.

LIZ: This is the smoker's table, isn't it.

MARK: I think you can smoke anywhere outside really, but this is where people come, innit, yeah.

LIZ: Sort of behind the bikeshed I suppose. Behind the woodpile, anyway. And we all started doing it because it felt a bit naughty. Sex sex sex, isn't it.

MARK: What?

LIZ: Smoking. I don't know where sex stops and smoking begins.

MARK: No?

LIZ: Cos you start to become sexualised, don't you. When you're growing up, you start to feel – but you don't realise maybe that that's what's happening. Not straight away. All you know is you want to do something – I don't know, you feel – and there's this ban on tobacco advertising, so that must be naughty, right? So maybe you wanna do that. And James Dean's always smoking, and you just know he's shagged every night, and deep down you know it's about getting laid really, you do know, so they sort of get –

MARK: Linked in your head.

LIZ: That's it! And there's all the – I don't know, there's a sort of phallic aspect isn't there? Look at that. Of course a penis is bigger than that, in most cases, but all the same. Do you want one?

MARK: You're all right.

LIZ: Or maybe it's more about nipples, I don't know. Maybe fags are like, a flight from sexuality, maybe it's wanting to get back to sucking on nipples, while you're growing up, after a ride, so you get something to put in your mouth. And it's not a cock, it's a thumb to suck. But on fire. I'm Liz by the way.

MARK: Oh. Mark.

LIZ: Hi Mark. Sorry, I – mm. Sure you don't want one?

MARK: Actually would you mind?

LIZ: Course not.

MARK: Thanks.

They light up.

LIZ: God, I was gasping. I don't like to smoke in the car. I volunteer for Contact the Elderly, do you know them?

MARK: Erm –

LIZ: They had some very good adverts about two years ago, sort of riffing on *When Harry Met Sally*, do you remember them?

MARK: I don't think so.

LIZ: Anyway, that was how I heard about them. They're great. Their thing is that older people get very isolated, very alone, so they arrange these tea parties. And you can volunteer either to host one where you live or to drive the elderly people to and from these parties, and stay with them while they're there to make sure they're all right.

MARK: Nursery school for old people.

LIZ: Yeah, I suppose. Anyway, I live in a shoe box so I can't have people round, but I can drive, so I volunteer for that bit, which I love. But the trouble is it means I don't like to smoke in my car, or it stinks of fags and I worry they'll think I'm degenerate, or choke to death on second hand smoke. So whenever I get to the end of a drive I'm always gasping.

MARK: Right.

LIZ: You don't smoke usually?

MARK: No. I always thought I'd smoke when I grew up, cos my Dad did –

LIZ: Then it killed him?!

MARK: It did actually, yeah.

LIZ: Oh God I'm so sorry.

MARK: No, but it wasn't that that stopped me.

LIZ: No?

MARK: It was the smoking ban, really. You know? Cos my idea
of smoking couldn't actually come true, like, by the time
I started earning enough money to buy any fags. So there
didn't seem much point in it. Yeah. There you go, that's
how it goes, isn't it.

LIZ: Little bit of your cultural inheritance robbed from you.

MARK: Yeah.

LIZ: Is it true they're putting the war memorial back up today?

MARK: What?

LIZ: Well I'm playing for this funeral this morning. I'm the
organist for the church, you see. And this funeral, it's
this girl from round here who drove her car into the war
memorial and died last week. So sad. She was back from
university and driving too fast, and apparently she didn't
have her car with her in London so she hadn't been driving
for a few months and she was out of practise and she sort
of lost control. It's so sad isn't it. I don't think they should
let such young people on the roads, they can't be trusted.
It's a wonder she didn't hurt anyone else. But anyway, the
vicar told me when I was parking my car, I always park
my car there first then have my fag here and a lemonade to
spruce up because I don't like smoking near the church in
case Jesus sees me, the vicar said there's actually going to
be work being done on the war memorial today, while the
bloody hearse goes by! They'll be putting it back together
while she gets driven past, how tasteless is that?

MARK: Right.

LIZ: Did you know her, the girl who died? Are you from round
here at all?

Enter JOHN with three drinks.

JOHN: An Englishman, an Irishman, a Scotsman, a Dutchman, a Belgian, a Welsh bloke, a Frenchman, a German, a Spaniard, an Uruguayan, a Brazilian, an American, a Canadian mounted policeman, an Indian, an Australian, a Kiwi, a Peruvian, a Slovenian, a Russian, an Ukrainian and a Chinaman walk up to a nightclub, and the doorman says sorry gents, you can't come in. Why not? They all ask. The doorman shrugs. Because you haven't got a Thai. Thank God for cheeky beers.

MARK: Cheers.

LIZ: That was actually much less racist than I expected it to be, John, well done. You can keep that one.

JOHN: No, they're like mayflies, jokes. I keep 'em for one day only. After that they're yours to cherish and disseminate or otherwise discard.

LIZ: Well I obviously never tell any of them to anyone I know.

JOHN: Why not?

LIZ: Without being a nun or anything I have sort of constructed a persona that doesn't really leave room for blow job jokes.

JOHN: The ferret joke isn't a blow job joke. It's a subversive exploration of the prejudices of its audience.

LIZ: Is it.

MARK: It's a beautiful snowflake.

JOHN: It feints with one overextended comic situation then surprises the listener with a different joke about chauvinist conceptions of women. And in the laughter or the silence it prompts in the listener, which is more genuine and honest thanks to the element of surprise that comes by way of building up the first dummy joke, it invites said listener to learn something about themselves and their own preconceptions.

LIZ: It's not, it's a blowjob joke. You're a tosser, John, but I like you for trying to talk your way out. Should you be drinking this early?

JOHN: No.

LIZ: You will anyway?

JOHN: Yup.

LIZ: I tell him every week but I don't think he believes in liver failure, he thinks it's like the tooth fairy or the female orgasm.

JOHN: I always start with a cheeky beer about now. Then six or eight of those and then a bit of rosé, maybe a bottle of rosé for the afternoon, then VATs for the evening.

LIZ: VATs?

MARK: Vodka and tonic.

LIZ: Christ, John.

JOHN: It's a lot, isn't it.

LIZ: It's quite a lot. How many vodka and tonics you drink?

JOHN: Sometimes six. Sometimes sixteen.

MARK: I suppose you're a big enough bloke like.

LIZ: You shouldn't do that to yourself.

JOHN: I can hold it. You should stick around some time, you'll find I become quite talkative.

LIZ: I find you quite talkative enough.

MARK: Do you need so much, to feel it then?

JOHN: No, not really. It just helps, is all.

LIZ: How?

JOHN: Well I think there's some comfort in being able to put your finger on precisely what your problem is, you know?

Get your feelings into boxes. If I was just existentially mournful that'd be awful, but because I've got a drinking problem...

LIZ: You've arranged yourself a drinking problem so you can have something concrete to feel depressed about?

JOHN: Exactly. No, I just like a drink really. And it's all free for me, isn't it. At the point of delivery. My little alcoholic NHS in there.

LIZ: Why do you think you're depressed?

JOHN: My wife left me.

LIZ: Oh John.

JOHN: What?

LIZ: You tell such terrible –

JOHN: No, she –

LIZ: Seriously?

JOHN: Yeah.

LIZ: Is he joking?

MARK: Erm –

LIZ: John, I'm so sorry.

JOHN: Nearly a year ago now.

LIZ: Oh fuck. That's why I never see her around any more?

JOHN: That'd probably be it.

LIZ: I thought she must have lie-ins on Sundays or something.

JOHN: No. Not here anyway. Possibly she has lie-ins in Marlborough with her new antique dealing boyfriend.

LIZ: A year?

JOHN: Yeah, been a while now. It's all over really, bar the attention-seeking suicide attempt. Divorce papers an' everythin'. Scrawl on the line. I've written the first fifty thousand words of an agony memoir about it.

LIZ: I've come here every month for two years and you've never said anything.

JOHN: Well it's not something you bring up, is it, really. And you never come in the pub, they all have a laugh about it in there, but you have your drink out here, and I'm not gonna bring you a lemonade and tell you a thing like that. My wife left me. Sounds like an awful chatup line. You might think I was trying it on!

LIZ: I just feel so awful.

JOHN: I bet you do. I've been on the market for a year, you haven't been buyin'. Not that I'd charge, not for you anyway.

LIZ: Oh, John.

JOHN: What? What?

Silence.

MARK: You must get proper fuckin' hangovers drinking that much, right John?

JOHN: I think I'm always just a bit pissed. Specially now. What with. It was already happening before she left, that was how I knew she wasn't making it up. She said something about me and the drink when she left. No, that's unfair. She was clearer than that, I'm being unfair. She said I wasn't the man she'd married any more, and I hadn't been for a long time, and this wasn't the life she'd thought we'd have, and it never had been. And she said she'd turned fifty and it'd made her think, and if she didn't do something with her life now, she'd never be able to live with herself. Cos when the day came that her legs stopped working all she'd have to entertain herself with would be this, us, and it wasn't enough for her. And she said she'd decided she was never going to do anything living with me. Then she told me I drank too much. Then she told me she was sorry. Then she told me I ought to look after myself. Then she left. I had to look at myself and say I suppose you haven't been happy for a long time either. Anyway.

MARK: Fuck mate.

JOHN: Yeah.

LIZ: That's so beautiful.

JOHN: What?

LIZ: I mean it's sad. Beautiful and sad. Same thing.

JOHN: That's a weird little insight into your head right there.

LIZ: Is it? Don't you think the way things sort of just, happen to people, you know?

MARK: You getting a decent send off?

JOHN: Not really. People are keeping away.

MARK: Why?

LIZ: Where are you going?

JOHN: Away. I've sold up.

LIZ: What?

JOHN: My soon to be ex-wife wanted her half of everything. Which is her right, and which she's more than earned, I reckon. So I had to sell up. No money for buying her out of the pub.

LIZ: Fuck.

JOHN: It's all right.

LIZ: No, fuck. Are you all right?

JOHN: Course.

LIZ: Today?

JOHN: I know.

MARK: Why hasn't anyone been round to say goodbye?

JOHN: I don't know mate, do I. I only know they haven't come. I like to think of it as a reminder. Any time I've thought I was anything more than a service to people I've been fooling myself. All I am and ever have been is a supplier of alcoholic products. Which is good for me in a way, keeps me grounded. People don't feel emotional connections to pubs, not really. They say they do, but. They're places to pass through, places to drink in. Or if people do feel emotional connections, it's nothing to do with me. The pub was standing long before I was standing in it, it'll be here long after I'm gone, I'm not really important to the operation, am I. I just lived here for a little while. What matters is the people who drink here, not the people who run it.

LIZ: There are people who'd say you're the life and soul of the place.

JOHN: You might say that. I couldn't possibly comment. But no one's dropped in to say goodbye, so I think you're in a minority.

LIZ: God.

JOHN: I think maybe once you know something's closing it starts to look sick. People maybe steer clear of a place once its notice is posted, in case they catch something. Catch closing time, sort of thing. And apart from anything else I think people are boycotting because I'm selling to the man.

LIZ: No.

MARK: What man?

JOHN: You know.

MARK: No.

LIZ: The / man the man.

JOHN: You know, the man! Don't you say that? Maybe that's gone out of fashion. Christ I feel old talking to you. Look, this pub's never been part of a chain before, has it. Obviously. Nothing's ever been part of a chain round here. And I won't feel guilty, cos there just aren't people looking to buy pubs anywhere, and if you have to sell you have to sell to who's buying, but I do feel ashamed in a way. Letting a chain in here. Because a pub's a business, sure, you have to make money, you have to pay your bills, but it's supposed to be more than that isn't it. It's much more than that. You have responsibilities. To the soul of a place. Because there is such a thing as society. It happens here, I see it every evening. And here I am monetising conviviality.

MARK: I wouldn't beat yourself up mate. It'll still be selling the same drinks, won't it.

LIZ: And no one's going to blame you if you didn't have a choice.

JOHN: It's about sameness, though, isn't it. People like us, we're supposed to live – I don't know. What would you say? In defiance of cultural homogeny. That's what living in the country means. We don't just live here, do we, it's a philosophy, it's an argument we're making.

LIZ: Yes exactly. That's exactly what it is, I've always thought that. We believe in long walks and cold showers and early mornings.

JOHN: Well –

MARK: I don't think that's true.

LIZ: No?

MARK: I think that's true if you can afford it. If. Far as I see, living here means keeping your head above water. Or fighting to. And failing, and moving to town, and all that breaking your heart. And no money and damp in the bedroom and taking a third or fourth job just to stay where you are, like, cos you only know this life you were born to, don't you, and you don't want to change it. And no, no one's going to bed at night praying for – I don't know, an All You Can Eat Buffet, but it's not so different from what you do, so I wouldn't feel too bad mate.

LIZ: Sorry.

MARK: What?

LIZ: I'm sorry.

MARK: Right.

LIZ: I didn't mean to upset you.

MARK: I'm not fucking upset.

Silence.

JOHN: I like you Marky Mark. You're like me.

MARK: Am I?

JOHN: We've got things in common, see Liz, him and me.

LIZ: Yeah?

JOHN: We've both lost women we love.

LIZ: Oh –

MARK: Do you think so?

JOHN: What?

MARK: Do you think we're in the same boat there? Fuck's sake. You had the chance to love her. I just had a few years when I used to know a girl who was too good for me. You had the chance to love her. She'll be too good for me for ever now. I'll never have – well I never will have – well. Fuck's sake.

Silence.

JOHN: I'm sorry Mark.

MARK: No, no.

JOHN: No, but I am. I'm being –

MARK: It's all right.

JOHN: You're right. Yeah. I'm sorry. You're right. I didn't have a chance to make her change her mind, though. I had no say in her decision to take away the meaning of my life. Like that. Just like that. I'm gonna go in.

LIZ: Stay a minute.

JOHN: Why?

LIZ: I don't know. I'm just –

JOHN: I need to get to work really.

LIZ: Are you all right? Will you be all right?

JOHN: I'm all right.

LIZ: Maybe I'll drop round later. We could talk some more.

JOHN: What about?

LIZ: I don't know. If you wanted to talk about how you were feeling.

JOHN: Oh, right. That's not really something I go in for to be honest.

LIZ: OK. Well the offer's there.

JOHN: All right. See you later Mark.

MARK: Yeah all right. I'm sorry John. I didn't mean –

JOHN: I know. At least you're talking to me. Since she left no one talks to me about anything any more. Least of all about her. It's like everyone's trying to keep a secret. Trouble is the secret's out. I'm going in. You two gonna be all right?

MARK: Yeah.

JOHN: Liz?

LIZ: Me? Yes I'm fine. I ought to be going, really. Don't want to be late.

JOHN: I suppose you're not going? To the –

MARK: No. Can't, can I.

JOHN: All right. I have to start on lunch.

Exit JOHN.

MARK: What was that all about?

LIZ: What?

MARK: Your little rendezvous.

LIZ: I just think he might want someone to talk to.

MARK: Oh yeah.

LIZ: I just think he might need some help, is all. He's a kind man, you know. Under all that. He's not actually a wanker. I don't think. He always brings me my drink. I think he looks after me, you know.

MARK: Why do you need looking after?

LIZ: No, I don't mean – I don't need that. I don't need anyone to look after me. Is that the funeral you said you couldn't go to?

MARK: Yeah.

LIZ: You did know her then.

MARK: Yeah.

LIZ: Oh. I'm sorry. I hope I didn't say anything –

MARK: No you're all right.

LIZ: Sometimes I talk too much.

MARK: It's because of the centenary, innit.

LIZ: What?

MARK: That's why there's been a rush to get the memorial done. We're having events like everywhere else. Hundred years on sort of thing. Boo hoo. So the council want it fixed quick as poss cos it's supposed to be part of all the events, see? Something to march past. Trouble is, what maybe looks like a sensible decision at council level, the war memorial's fallen down, let's get it back up again sharpish, always looks a bit different to the people on the ground, you're right. What looks efficient on a meeting agenda looks sort of fucking tasteless when she gets driven past the road works, that's true. And the worst of it is that out here, what starts as a council policy always ends up as a local taking a day's work doing something he wishes he didn't have to, cos he doesn't know how else he's going to pay his rent. So yeah, I know quite a lot about the war memorial getting fixed. It's me that's doing it.

LIZ: Oh.

MARK: I don't want to. She was my best friend. I felt that anyway. She had a lot of friends, but she was *my* best friend. We lived next to each other. Grew up together. But I have to take the work, see. Round here there's little enough before you start turning stuff down on principle. From the fuckin' council an all. You don't wanna be on their blacklist.

LIZ: I'm so sorry.

MARK: I feel so sad about it. Cos she used to let me hold her hand, you know? And I can still feel what that felt like. You know? Yeah.

LIZ: I really didn't mean to be rude. I feel awful.

MARK: You weren't rude. I'm fuckin' furious about it. But I've been a motorway repairman and slept five nights a week in my cab by the side of the road, I've chipped the mortar off bricks while the snow was falling. You do the work, that's all, you do the work there is and pay the rent and pay the rent. There's no say in it. You have to take your work where you can find it. You ought to go, you know. It won't be long before people start arriving. Fuckin' flowers everywhere I suppose, all round the church.

LIZ: Yes. Flowers everywhere. I don't want to leave you like this.

MARK: Like what?

LIZ: You know. I don't know. Sad.

MARK: I don't really think there's anything you can say that's going to do much about that.

LIZ: Right. No. Of course. Well perhaps I'll –

MARK: He's all right you know, John. If you were looking for a character reference. He's all right.

LIZ: It's nothing like that. I just thought he might need a friend, OK?

MARK: All right. Just saying. Nice to meet you.

LIZ: And you. Perhaps I'll see you later.

MARK: Well you'll know where to find me. I'll be putting the memorial back up.

SCENE TWO

JOHN is sitting on the bench, a crown on his head, a pewter tankard in his hands. He sits. He looks into the tankard. It's got a glass bottom, and he waves his hand under it then sits up and looks out as if it's a telescope. He cries. Enter LIZ.

JOHN: *(Sings.)* And it's no, nay, never, no nay never no more, and I'll play the wild rover, no never, no more.

LIZ: John?

115

JOHN: Oh. Sorry. I was –

LIZ: What's the matter?

She sits by him.

JOHN: They all turned up.

LIZ: Who?

JOHN: For the wake of course, they were having the wake here. The whole village. And then –

LIZ: What?

JOHN: Bill Owen, do you know Bill? Oldest buffer here. Father of the village, if you will. Or he likes to act like he is. Lives along in one of the cottages, he's been there since about forty-eight, he's gone ninety. You might not know him, he doesn't go to church. Bill stands up and the place falls silent. The whole village is looking at him. And he says we all know today is a sad day, today is Lucy's day, but there's someone else who's leaving us this evening, and the number of times I've seen Lucy drunk in here I don't think she'd want to let it pass without comment. And he raises a toast to me. To the rest of my life. And the boys get out this cava and spray it all over me, and stick this fucking crown on my head, and say they reckon Lucy would have wanted to join in with that and all. Then Bill gives me this tankard, look. For a present. Look. 'To John, from his friends in the village.' And I just cried. I couldn't help it. I didn't know what to say. I didn't say anything.

LIZ: That's lovely. I think that's lovely.

JOHN: I thought they were keeping away. To show what they thought about things.

LIZ: Of course they weren't keeping away. You will have been loved by people here John, you know all that stuff you were spouting this morning was bollocks. You will have been loved.

JOHN: I thought I'd let them down, is all.

LIZ: You haven't done anything like that. You've done what you must. That's all right. People understand that. *(JOHN cries.)* Hey, hey. Don't cry. OK. Come here. Don't cry. Come on. *(A silence while JOHN recovers himself.)* Well. It must have been a funny note to strike at a wake.

JOHN: I suppose so. I might have one more drink, d'you want one?

LIZ: Not for me, thanks, no.

JOHN: Fair enough. *(He starts looking for a bottle.)* It felt sort of good, though, really. When you thought about things. To raise a glass to something. Because she was lovely, you know? Did you know her?

LIZ: No.

JOHN: I'd have thought she was in your choir. She was a good singer.

LIZ: We don't have a choir, John. Shows how often you go to church.

JOHN: Last time I went there was a choir.

LIZ: That was a concert. I was sitting in front of you, that was some students singing *Acis and Galatea*, that wasn't a choir.

JOHN: I don't know the difference really. It's all singing, innit. Anyway it didn't seem so wrong this afternoon. Her mum and dad were both there, I think they were happy when Bill stood up. Take the attention away, you know? Everyone looking at them and no one knowing what to say. It's such a sad thing, but she was lovely, so it felt sort of good to smile about something.

LIZ: To be a bit happy.

JOHN: Only because she always seemed happy.

LIZ: I know.

JOHN: When you're the bright one or the beautiful one in a place as small as this it stands out, you know? You matter to everyone. In towns, even if you're a genius, you're only ever really a drop in the ocean. We were all proud of her here. Even me, even us outsiders.

LIZ: You weren't an outsider, you were the life and soul of the place.

JOHN: For a little while, yeah.

He has found several beer bottles, but all of them are empty.

JOHN: Oh, fuck. I thought I'd brought enough to last me a while.

He blows on one to make the empty bottle noise.

LIZ: How long have you been out here?

JOHN: Dunno. A while. That's probably why – yeah, right. I'm so fucking hot, you know?

LIZ: Oh John.

JOHN: Sweating like a fat lad.

He blows on two of the other bottles.

LIZ: Look at you.

JOHN: This one isn't finished though.

LIZ: Don't drink it John.

JOHN: What?

LIZ: You've had enough, haven't you.

JOHN: Have I?

LIZ: I think you've had enough.

JOHN: Right. OK. I see.

He puts the bottle down.

JOHN: Don't go calling me a fuckin' alkie, yeah?

LIZ: I'm not, I promise.

JOHN: Cos people get shocked with how much I drink, but I'm all right, you know? I drink two litres of water at bedtime. My kidneys are fine. I got em checked. I don't get the shakes. I can handle my drink.

LIZ: All right.

JOHN: And if you're thinking this is the classic aggressive behaviour of the alcoholic in denial, you can fuck yourself an all, yeah?

He starts taking his shirt off.

LIZ: Do you need to undress now, John?

JOHN: Nah, it's fine. Hot, that's all. You're making a face like it's not fine.

LIZ: I just think we were talking, and now you're taking your clothes off, really.

JOHN: All right, it's all right. Don't worry about it.

He takes off his shirt. He is wearing a t shirt underneath.

JOHN: STELLA!!!

LIZ laughs.

JOHN: Good right? I'm a dead ringer aren't I.

LIZ: For the later Marlon Brando, maybe.

JOHN: Look at this.

He grabs the umbrella for the picnic table and hoists the shirt atop as a flag.

LIZ: What are you doing?

JOHN: Hang on.

LIZ: Be careful.

JOHN: Who are you, my Mum? Look at that!

LIZ: What is it?

JOHN: Well it's a flag, innit. Jolly Roger.

LIZ: It doesn't have a skull and cross bones.

JOHN: No. Not the Jolly Roger then. I suppose we'll just have to do all the rogering ourselves, boom boom!

LIZ: Funny.

JOHN: You know me. Always ready with a one liner. I'd never have believed my father was stealing from his job as a road mender, but I went round his flat the other day and the signs are all there. Boom boom!

LIZ: You're like, half Bruce Forsyth and half Basil Brush, what's happened to you?

JOHN: My brother's addicted to brake fluid, but he says he can stop at any time.

LIZ laughs.

JOHN: This cafe had a sign in the window advertising breakfast at any time, so I went in and asked for French toast during the Renaissance.

LIZ laughs again.

JOHN: I like your laugh.

LIZ: Thank you.

JOHN: I'm pleased you liked my jokes.

LIZ: I sort of felt carpet bombed into submission.

JOHN: I think they call it clusterfucking.

LIZ: Sounds exhausting.

JOHN: Boom boom. Christ, I'm out of breath. Strenuous brilliance, that's what tires me out.

LIZ: All right?

JOHN: Yeah, yeah.

LIZ: So you're actually selling tonight then are you? This is actually it, your last evening? And the man's turning up for the keys tomorrow morning?

JOHN: That's it.

LIZ: God.

JOHN: Weird, innit.

LIZ: I'm so gutted.

JOHN: Why?

LIZ: I don't know. I'm just sad.

JOHN: Gonna miss me?

LIZ: Oh, John.

JOHN: Sad for me you mean.

LIZ: For you, but. I don't know. I've felt like we were getting to know each other, you know? In the time I've been coming here. And I've enjoyed how that's been taking its time, cos I thought we were going to be doing this for years, I thought there was lots of time to, to take. I thought there was loads of chat to look forward to. But you're off.

JOHN: Right. I suppose.

LIZ: You'll definitely go?

JOHN: Yeah.

LIZ: D'you know where yet?

JOHN: No.

LIZ: Mm.

JOHN: What?

LIZ: Could you not stay here? And still be part of it?

JOHN: In the village?

LIZ: Yeah.

JOHN: I don't think I could go and pay for my drinks in there. And what would I do for work anyway? All fucking horrible jobs everyone does round here to make ends meet.

LIZ: That's what drags me out here on a Sunday.

JOHN: How d'you mean?

LIZ: No other jobs. Nowhere any nearer home I can get the gig playing the organ. I'm not any great shakes at it, to be honest, see, so all the bigger places nearer by, nearer my home, they don't want me. Two hours I drive to play here, cos it's the only place that'll have me. It's a crappy little organ. I think they might have scrapped it by now if I didn't keep turning up. So I suppose in a way I keep the habit up for the whole place, singing with an organ, I mean. Which I think is nice.

JOHN: I'm sure everyone appreciates it.

LIZ: Labour of love you know. Twenty quid in petrol money's all they can give.

JOHN: How much does the petrol cost for the drive?

LIZ: Twenty-five quid.

JOHN: That's good. That's very neat.

LIZ: Yeah, I know.

JOHN: Bit colder only wearing a vest.

LIZ: I bet. So this is your last night.

JOHN: Actually last night was my last night really. I think on the forms it says ownership transfers at closing time. I don't even know if I'm allowed to sleep here. I'm going to. Bloke who's having it off me only works nine to five, he won't get here till the morning. And I'll spend tomorrow moving out, there hasn't been time yet. They understand all that. They know it's weird. So I have one more night in there.

LIZ: What will you do with it?

JOHN: I dunno. Probably cry into this funny little tankard.

LIZ: Well that sounds fun.

JOHN: Not to be missed. Why do you do it? The organ playing. If you don't mind me asking.

LIZ: Well it's fun isn't it. And it's only once a month, with the way the services work out.

JOHN: No, but why do you actually do it?

LIZ: What do you mean?

JOHN: Why this and not watercolour painting? Or dogging or whatever.

LIZ: I guess because I believe in it.

JOHN: In God?

LIZ: No, you don't have to believe in God to be an Anglican. That's the whole point. The right to have an equivocal relationship with everything, that's the point. I mean the ritual. And the songs. Some of them are really good songs. It's what we're all brought up with, isn't it. It's where we're all from. I think you have to pay some heed to that. Or someone does. Or I do, anyway.

JOHN: I'm sure people are grateful that you do.

LIZ: I'm sure they're not, I'm sure it never crosses their mind. But if – well imagine that who we are is the sum total of everything that's ever happened to us, right?

JOHN: Right.

LIZ: Well if that's true, if that was true, then I think old ceremonies must be important, because of that. And the church. The church is big you know? Big thing. It's part of the reason for almost everything that's happened, isn't it. Cos everyone ever like, used to read the Bible. All the time. So it's in us, isn't it. Part of. Even the Beatles went to Sunday school, you know?

JOHN: Sure.

LIZ: And people say the church doesn't matter any more. And I think those people can sod off, to be honest, because it makes me so angry to hear someone dismiss another person's culture. And it's bollocks and all. Because it's still who we are, even if we ignore it. And I'm not saying it's a good thing or a bad thing, it's just a fact, it's who we are.

JOHN: As long as you don't think it's an unbridled joy, I can go along with that.

LIZ: No, no. It does terrible bloody damage, the church. But you fix things by getting to the cause, not burying it. And now Rowan Williams tells me we live in a post-Christian society and I think, hang on a minute. Because that's my culture you're attacking, and seeing as you were running the fucking joint a year ago it really ought to be yours to defend as well. And who the hell are all the bishops sitting unelected in the Lords if we live in a post-Christian culture anyway? It's not the truth because look what the Queen's in charge of. He's probably just being paid to run the thing down cos someone wants to buy it.

JOHN: What's your favourite hymn then?

LIZ: What?

JOHN: Go on, you must have a favourite.

LIZ: No!

JOHN: Any hymn.

LIZ: *Praise my Soul The King of Heaven* then, I like that. Oh no, *Abide With Me. Abide With Me.* Played that this afternoon. They're by the same guy you know.

JOHN: Yeah?

LIZ: Henry Francis Lyte. Isn't that a lovely name? Actually there's a beautiful story about *Abide With Me*.

JOHN: Go on.

LIZ: Well Lyte was the curate of All Saints Church in Brixham, in Devon. By the sea. And he'd got ill, right? TB. And it was decided he should move to Italy. For his health, they used to think that helped, the climate and whatever. And after he preached for the last time in his church, he'd been there for twenty-seven years, he preached for the last time, and when he was done he went down to the sea. It's like Matthew Arnold, it's like *Dover Beach*. Ah love, let us be true to one another, you know? And while he was on the beach, he had this moment of, I don't know, this inspiration. And he wrote *Abide With Me*. And two weeks later he was dead.

JOHN: No way.

LIZ: Died in Nice on the way down to Italy. But the lovely thing, right, the lovely thing is that you can go down to Brixham and at eight every evening when the light's going out of the sky, in summer anyway, it's dark in the winter of course, but at the same time every evening they play the tune on the church bells. Isn't that lovely?

JOHN: That's lovely. Yeah. Have you been then?

LIZ: No, I just heard about it from a teacher in Salisbury I knew. I wanna go. I just haven't got round to it yet. They did it at the funeral, *Abide With Me*. That was one of the hymns.

JOHN: Oh yeah?

LIZ: Actually I don't like *Abide With Me* best.

JOHN: No?

LIZ: No. If I have to pick one, if I have to pick one it has to be *Dear Lord and Father of Mankind*.

JOHN: That's a good one.

LIZ: You know it?

JOHN sings the first verse of 'Dear Lord and Father of Mankind', and LIZ joins in and sings it with him.

LIZ: Isn't that lovely?

JOHN: Yeah, that's a good one. You know your organ playing?

LIZ: What?

JOHN: Your organ playing.

LIZ: What about it?

JOHN: Well –

LIZ: Go on.

JOHN: Well sometimes I think when I hear people talking a lot, that what they're actually trying to do is not say what's really on their mind. What's actually getting to them.

LIZ: Oh.

JOHN: I was listening to you. Been listening. 'Bout keeping cultures alive or whatever. And I just don't buy it, really. I don't think people act out of such – cos I think you're not happy, Liz, put simply. That's what I think. And I don't think anything happens that isn't about feeling love or lack of love for another person, which might just be me, but that's what I think, so all the time I've been listening to you talk I've been getting this picture. Of a man you don't know any more you wish you still knew. I believe in that much more as an explanation for who you are than the one you've just given me. You mustn't mind me saying this. It's my last day, I want to be honest with you.

LIZ: Right.

JOHN: Am I wrong?

126

LIZ: You're telling your own story, John, not mine, that's all.

JOHN: My assessment of you –

LIZ: Go on.

JOHN: My assessment of you has always basically been that you're someone who needs to get laid.

LIZ: Excuse me?

JOHN: Don't you think? I think there's a sexual element in everything, I think that's what it is. I think everything is sex.

LIZ: That's very definitely your story, not mine.

JOHN: Maybe. But that's how I see you.

LIZ: Well you can fuck off then John.

JOHN: What?

LIZ: You div.

JOHN: All I'm / trying to say –

LIZ: I was being nice. I was trying to distract you, that's all. From how you were feeling, and you can fuck off do I need to get laid. Of course I need to get laid, don't we all, that's not who I bloody am!

JOHN: Right.

LIZ: God's sake!

JOHN: Sorry.

LIZ: Don't bother, all right? Fuck's sake.

JOHN: I'm sorry. All I was trying to say was that I wanted to kiss you.

LIZ: Right. I see. I'm going to go now.

JOHN: Oh. / You don't –

LIZ: I was only trying to be nice. I suppose you're unstable because of your wife.

JOHN: I'm not –

LIZ: You're such an idiot. You're such a fucking idiot. I've so liked talking to you, out here, our little chats, I've always looked forward to them. Never expecting anything to – come of it, that was what was so – because you had a wife, you were someone I could just talk to, you were finally someone to talk to. But you don't have a wife. Do you. And here I am. And I thought – I've always thought. All you had to do was not fuck it up, John, because I've thought the world of you all the time I've been driving out here. And now you've fucked it up. There you go. That's that. I'm going to go. I'm going to go. Good luck in the future John, all right? Whatever you do with it. Have a good life.

JOHN: Liz.

LIZ: I have to go. Good bye. I – good bye.

JOHN: Liz –

LIZ exits. JOHN sits alone. He hears someone coming, and stops, embarrassed.

Enter MARK.

MARK: All right.

JOHN: All right.

MARK puts his tool kit down.

JOHN: You done then?

Silence.

MARK: How was the –?

MARK sits.

MARK: Was that that funny woman from the church?

JOHN: Leave it will you Mark? Let it remain as a beautiful snowflake.

SCENE THREE

MARK is wearing a suit. He has a fag. Enter LIZ, also dressed smartly.

LIZ: I know you, don't I?

MARK: Scuse me?

LIZ: Haven't we met before?

MARK: Last year. I –

LIZ: That's it.

MARK: You're the organist.

LIZ: That's me. Liz.

MARK: Mark.

LIZ: Yes. Hello again Mark. Isn't it a beautiful day?

MARK: Yeah.

LIZ: This is a lovely village in the sun.

MARK: Yeah.

LIZ: I'm excited, seeing it on a Saturday. I don't usually come up here Saturdays, but there's a wedding.

MARK: Yeah.

LIZ: It's your wedding?

MARK: Yeah.

LIZ: Congratulations! That's lovely. That's so lovely. How are you feeling?

MARK: Yeah. I mean. It's pretty –

LIZ: It's the same for everyone, don't worry. I've done a lot of weddings. All the grooms I see, it's a big day.

MARK: Yeah.

LIZ: A happy day, but you get scared as well.

MARK: Exactly.

LIZ: Because in theory, this is the last person you'll ever shag, isn't it. And I know for a man that's quite –

MARK: I'm not worried about that.

LIZ: No? Well that's good then.

MARK: Yeah.

LIZ: Just the bloody magnitude of it.

MARK: Loads of things. I, erm. Actually. I don't know whether I can do it, actually.

LIZ: How d'you mean?

MARK: I just don't know – I don't know if I can do it.

LIZ: Oh right.

MARK: I just thought I'd hide for a minute, you know, just –

LIZ: Right. That's why you're –

MARK: No one really comes round here, yeah. It's a bit like. Horrible. I don't know –

LIZ: Do you want me to / leave you alone?

MARK: No, no, it might be good to have someone to – I'm just scared, you know? Really – it's so weird like. And I can't talk to any of my mates, I can't.

LIZ: What's up?

MARK: It feels quite fast, you know? It feels quite fast. And I don't want to make a mistake. Cos I'd hurt her, if I was, and I couldn't bear it, you know? Cos she's amazing. I love her, you know? Only it feels quite fast.

LIZ: When did you meet?

MARK: Years back. School, like. She was below me in school. I sort of knew her, not properly but. But we started seeing each other like, nine months ago.

LIZ: OK. That's not so fast if everything's wonderful?

MARK: Yeah, and everything is, everything is wonderful. But I feel so lucky, you know? I can't believe my luck, that someone wanted me. So I feel like I'm pushing my luck. This. And I didn't think this would ever, ever happen to me, and it's now it's fucking happening today, and you're like – fuck.

LIZ: Right, yeah.

MARK: So that's it really.

LIZ: Right. What are you gonna do?

MARK: I dunno. My head's like.

LIZ: Yeah.

MARK: I keep thinking about all the things I thought I'd have done before I got married.

LIZ: Oh yeah?

MARK: Not big things. I don't mind not having done them, even. I never had a proper plan or. Just – you know. I don't think I ever thought it was the sort of thing that. It's so real, isn't it.

LIZ: What did you want to do? Before you got married, I mean.

MARK: Well nothing big or anything. I haven't been to Wembley yet.

LIZ: Wembley's quite big.

MARK: I wanted to have filled the bookshelf in my room.

LIZ: What with?

MARK: Books.

LIZ: Yeah, what books?

MARK: Oh, anything really. I'm not picky. Just books I'd read. Anything I could get in Sue Ryder. There's better stuff in charity shops than you'd think.

LIZ: And what else did you plan to have done?

MARK: I was going to see the world.

LIZ: But you haven't?

MARK: Not really. I had a bit of a disastrous attempt.

LIZ: Oh yes?

MARK: Yeah. I was going with a friend, round the world, you know, I was going to go travelling. This was years ago, this was when I was a teenager. Really looking forward to it. But they changed their mind about going with me, went round the world with someone else, my friend did.

LIZ: Nice.

MARK: Yeah. So I went on my own. And I spent about a week in India and it was just horrible, really, so I came home.

LIZ: Oh.

MARK: Yeah.

LIZ: And you'd planned to stay out longer?

MARK: Like six months, yeah.

LIZ: Well six months is a lot of time to spend on your own.

MARK: Yeah. I sometimes wish I'd stayed out there.

LIZ: Yeah?

MARK: Well I didn't get any refunds so it cost the same going for a week as it would have done going for half a year.

More or less. What with the extra flights and all. And I'd quit my job and they wouldn't give it back so –

LIZ: That's a shame.

MARK: And I did – I felt I'd failed a bit. And I do feel like I haven't lived now, now that I'm settling down here properly. Haven't really tested myself or anything.

LIZ: What was so horrible about India, do you mind me asking?

MARK: Oh, it's hard to explain. I saw a dog tear a cat in two.

LIZ: Right.

MARK: Creep up on it and shake it till it came apart. I saw this child, this naked child squatting down to take a shit on a big pile of other people's shit, and these school children passing just spat at it. And the little kid looked so ashamed.

LIZ: God.

MARK: And the beggars. Guys with their eyes gouged out, you know? And sewed back up. These little girls would come up and ask me to buy them powdered milk for their baby brothers, then take you in a shop and you'd get charged like twenty quid for a packet. And I knew it was a stitch up but I just had to do it cos when you go out at night, there are literally hundreds of people just lying down in the road to sleep. You know?

LIZ: That's awful.

MARK: I spent about three hundred quid on powdered milk, just in the one week. Thought I deserved it. I just thought, you cunt. Coming over here like it's an adventure. When it's these people's lives. You don't know a fucking thing about anything. You deserve to be taken for all you've got. That was my attempt at widening my horizons. That was that. I thought it was so disrespectful to be there like I was. Without contributing anything. Just staring at everything. So all the money I didn't spend on powdered milk I took into Thomas Cook, this beautiful Thomas Cook with beautiful air conditioning, and I spent all the money I had on a plane ticket home.

LIZ: You really didn't like it then.

MARK: I hated myself for being there. I was an extra in a Bollywood movie. But yeah. That was that, anyway. Yeah.

LIZ: And this friend who didn't go with you, that was your friend who died, was it?

MARK: What?

LIZ: I just thought you might be thinking of her, today. If she meant things to you.

MARK: Right. Yeah. God, do you remember that?

LIZ: Of course.

MARK: Right, yeah, of course. Well yeah, I suppose that's why I'm thinking of. It is a bit quick, isn't it.

LIZ: I don't know.

MARK: No?

LIZ: Well it depends on how you feel, doesn't it.

MARK: Yeah. I suppose so.

LIZ: It was a suicide, wasn't it, her death.

MARK: What?

LIZ: I thought it was a suicide.

MARK: No. No one ever said anything like that.

LIZ: Oh, I'm sorry.

MARK: She just hadn't driven her car for a year. She'd had a few drinks and she wasn't used to driving and she was going a bit fast and she lost control.

LIZ: How sad.

MARK: It wasn't a suicide.

LIZ: No, no.

MARK: Did someone tell you that?

LIZ: No! I'm just misremembering. I never quite knew the facts of the thing, and she was a student, wasn't she, and a lot of the time it's students who – and all I remembered was that she drove into the war memorial. I remember that, that phrase. And I'm just getting confused by language, I see it now. Because 'drove' seems like such a deliberate word, doesn't it? But of course it doesn't have to mean she did it deliberately.

MARK: It just means she was driving. She didn't do it on purpose.

LIZ: No. That's good then. I mean, not good, sad. But better than – you know.

MARK: Yeah. Anyway. Yeah.

The sound of singing from the front of the pub. They listen for a moment.

MARK: I never thought anyone would ever actually love me. And I think someone does. And I fucking love them. And I'm so scared of fucking it up because it's all come too soon after – yeah. You know what I mean.

LIZ: Of course. Well maybe you're being sensible. Maybe you're right. Or maybe you just have to suck it and see, you know? People start early at a wedding, don't they! Is the party afterwards here as well?

MARK: We'll end up here in the evening I reckon. We're going to the big house for the meal, like, the lunch. Place on your left when you drive in?

LIZ: There's a wall and a big gate?

MARK: The house is sort of behind a lot of trees, yeah. That's the main place here. And we're both from here, me and my – Rhiannon –

LIZ: 'My wife and I'!

MARK: Yeah. So we hired the lawn and we've got a marquee. They've done us a deal.

LIZ: And the weather's fine, so you've been lucky. Someone's smiling on this one!

MARK: I hope so.

LIZ: So it's a big old stately home, behind the wall?

MARK: Well, sort of. The actual house is only really fifteen years old.

LIZ: Oh?

MARK: There used to be a big house there before. Local MP lived in it. Nice enough bloke. Not sure about his politics. Anyway, one night there was this fire. Someone left a hob on or something, I don't know. And the whole place went up, and sort of collapsed in on itself. And the fire was so strong, so fierce, they never even found the bodies. The people who lived in the house. Whole family gone.

LIZ: God.

MARK: I know. After they'd finished with it as a crime scene, or whatever, the site got sold, and this property developer bought it. He'd made his money building blocks of flats in Bristol, and he wanted a place to live, so he rebuilt the house. Room for room, brick for brick, used the original plans, he lives there now with his family.

LIZ: And does he have anything to do with everyone? Or with the work here, with the farming?

MARK: Farming's all sold off to big outfits years ago. Big operations run all this now.

LIZ: Do they do sheep?

MARK: Some sheep, yeah.

LIZ: I like sheep. Some people say cows are nicer but I think they kill people who walk their dogs. It was all farming I suppose, all this village. Before everyone who lived here was an old age pensioner I mean. Everyone was a farmer. Shame.

MARK: I dunno. The people who lived here were more or less serfs.

LIZ: Yeah?

MARK: The big house paid out wages, but they took plenty back in rents, cos he owned all the cottages. Right? And the wages used to get paid out over the bar in the pub, so plenty got spent straight away in there. And the big house owned the pub as well. So in a way he never really spent any money on the people who worked for him. Just passed a few coins round till they came back into his hands a week later, one way or another.

LIZ: There must be books and books about it. Social history. People writing memoirs. 'Confessions of a shepherd' sort of thing.

MARK: I suppose there are.

LIZ: Do you have those sorts of books on your shelf, do you read about the country?

MARK: A bit. It's more spy novels really.

LIZ: Fair enough. I love a history book, me. The book I always think I'd like to read when I drive up over the chase is a history of road laying.

MARK: A history of road laying?

LIZ: No, it would be interesting! I'd love to know what everyone thought when all this tarmac started happening everywhere. Because that must have been such a shock to the psyche. Of the whole country. All those dirt tracks or whatever getting inked in for ever. It's like. It's like your war memorial isn't it.

MARK: My war memorial?

LIZ: The one you fixed. People live and die in villages like this all the time, don't they, and bit by bit the population of a village will change completely without anyone really noticing it. Like a body's cells are all replaced every seven years, is that right? But write some deaths into stone, you've got this much blunter portrait of a moment in time, you can't help but look at how a place has changed, can you.

MARK: Yeah.

LIZ: Well it's the same with roads for me. Surely for as long as roads were really just places where enough people had walked to make a track there must always have been a suspicion that they were invented, right? Like a dream. That enough people walking in a different direction could change the way a road went. But then you put down tarmac, and things are fixed for ever.

MARK: I suppose that might be an interesting book.

LIZ: I'm full of good ideas, me. I can always think of interesting books I could have written if only I'd been living at the right time. The trouble is we don't seem to be living through anything right now.

MARK: No?

LIZ: No, not really. I just mean it's hard to get things right while they happen to you isn't it. To see, clearly. That's what I think anyway. You're going to be my last gig here, you know.

MARK: Really?

LIZ: I have to stop doing it. Playing here, I mean. The organ. I'm pleased it's you who's getting married, it's nice that it's someone I know.

MARK: I'm gonna go through with it then am I?

LIZ: I was hoping I might be able to slip that in without you noticing.

MARK: Boom boom!

LIZ: *(Laughs.)* You're as bad as John.

MARK: I ought to be, I've got his job now.

LIZ: Have you?

MARK: Well, sort of. I'm the assistant manager.

LIZ: I didn't know that! God have I said anything rude about it? Only I do think the sexual politics of the calendars hanging in the loos are quite problematic, and sometimes I blurt things out.

MARK: No, you're all right.

LIZ: Thank God.

MARK: What's wrong with the calendars in the loos? It's just the local hunt doing *Calendar Girls*, it's all for charity.

LIZ: Yes, but you've had it open on the same month for about a year now, and I had a flick through and it's definitely because the girls from May 2013 have got the nicest arses.

MARK: Oh, yeah, they have. Is that bad?

LIZ: It is a bit bad, I think.

MARK: Sorry.

LIZ: Well, just something to think about maybe.

MARK: How come you're stopping playing the organ?

LIZ: Oh, lots of reasons. The organ's shot, for one thing, and they'll never afford to replace it.

MARK: No?

LIZ: Organs are expensive. And I don't know whether they should be much of a priority these days for churches.

MARK: Why not?

LIZ: I sort of think raising funds to help poor people or the elderly or whatever might be more important, you know? Is this what you want to be talking about, is this –

MARK: All I want to do is not talk about that. Just for a little bit longer.

LIZ: OK.

MARK: So will you tell me something else? Anything else. About why they shouldn't fix the organ, or whatever, I don't care, I'm not really listening, I just don't want to think.

LIZ: Sure. OK. Well, I don't think they ought to renew the organ because you know, music changes as well, you know, and I sometimes think a church trying to fix its organ runs the risk of looking stuck in the past. Because music changes. And God knows, it's my culture, I love organ music, and imagining the history of it, all the people who've sung the same hymns over the years, all the people over history brought together in a way by that, and even a year ago I thought it was all worth saving. I thought it was important it ought to be saved. But the world changes, doesn't it.

MARK: It does.

LIZ: And if people want drum kits in church perhaps they should be allowed them. It seems sad, somehow, but that's just me being stuck in the past, I should think. I'm talking too much about organs. You must need to get back to your people.

MARK: No, they know I wanted a minute.

LIZ: I think what I feel very conscious of is the fact that everything comes to an end, you see. A time always comes when it's time to move on. When I started coming here I was in quite a sad place, actually. Quite a sad bloody place. So I was looking for things to do, so I could drown out my spare time. And these days I feel much better about all that, so I don't think I need all the driving here and back as much.

MARK: What do you do for a living?

LIZ: I teach piano.

Enter JOHN.

JOHN: Hands off cocks, on socks!

LIZ: Oh.

MARK: Fucking hell, hello John!

JOHN: All right mate, how's tricks?

MARK: Good man, yeah. It's so good to see you!

JOHN: Course it is.

MARK: I didn't know whether you'd got your invitation.

JOHN: No?

MARK: You didn't reply to it.

JOHN: No?

MARK: I don't know whether there's a seat for you at lunch.

JOHN: Ah well. 'My bad', as the cool kids say. You'll be able to fit me in?

MARK: I dunno mate, to be honest. It's all like –

JOHN: I'll skip a course and come to the party. Sorry mate. Should have written back. Hello Liz, how are you?

He gives her a kiss on the cheek.

LIZ: Hello John.

JOHN: You look well.

LIZ: Thank you. So do you.

JOHN: Do I? Christ, imagine what I must have looked like when you saw me last. So you're having second thoughts are you?

MARK: What?

JOHN: Everyone knows, mate. Stands to reason. It's your wedding day and you're chain smoking round the back of the pub. Aren't they sweet, the young? They think it's all happening for the first time.

LIZ: Well it is for him.

JOHN: That's true. Mark, I want you to listen to me.

MARK: Right.

LIZ: John –

JOHN: It's all right. Mark. You have never believed you were worth much. But you always have been. You were shit at peeling potatoes when you used to work here, but everyone liked having you around. And you lost someone, very recently. But life goes on, mate. And here's someone standing with their hand out waiting for you. And you have to make a decision.

MARK: Right.

JOHN: Because things don't always happen at the pace we'd choose. So maybe this is all happening a little bit quickly. And it's hard to get your head round. But that's life, isn't it. And I suppose you have to ask yourself this. Do you want to try? Or would you rather never risk anything?

MARK: Right.

JOHN: You see what I mean, don't you.

MARK: Yeah.

JOHN: Well don't be a cunt then.

MARK: OK. Right. Yeah.

JOHN: Probably time to get down the church an all.

MARK: Is it? Oh Christ. I'd better go.

JOHN: Good man. Feel good?

MARK: Yeah. Yeah. I feel good. Yeah. Thanks.

JOHN: Fuck off.

MARK: Thanks Liz.

LIZ: Are you all right?

MARK: Yeah.

LIZ: Are you going to be all right?

MARK: Yeah. Yeah. I feel really good.

MARK exits.

JOHN: Sweet boy, isn't he.

LIZ: He's so frightened.

JOHN: So was I. Were you ever married?

LIZ: Yeah.

JOHN: What happened to your husband?

LIZ: He died.

JOHN: Oh, Liz.

LIZ: Yeah. Congenital cardiomyopathy.

JOHN: Fuck. I'm sorry.

LIZ: Me too. It was years ago now though. I was very scared as well.

JOHN: Yeah. I didn't know Liz, I'm sorry.

LIZ: You don't have anything to apologise for. I ought to get down the church if he's headed that way. It'd be typical me if the bride came up the aisle and I was still puffing my way up the hill. It's nice to see you.

JOHN: I hoped I'd see you.

LIZ: Oh yeah?

JOHN: Yeah.

LIZ: Well. We're lucky then aren't we.

JOHN: Yeah, I guess we are.

LIZ: I'd better make a start.

JOHN: Sure, of course. See you later maybe.

LIZ: OK.

JOHN: Bye then.

LIZ: Bye John. Bye.

LIZ exits.

SCENE FOUR

The evening of the wedding. Sound of a good night from the front of the pub. JOHN is sitting with a pint, staring into it. Enter MARK, lighting up.

MARK: So this is where you're hiding.

JOHN: I didn't know you smoked.

MARK: You all right?

JOHN: What?

MARK: Are you all right?

JOHN: Oh, you know me.

MARK: What does that mean?

JOHN: I'm all right.

MARK: All right.

JOHN: Yeah. So have you got my job here, then? Someone told me this is your gaffe now.

MARK: No, erm, assistant manager.

JOHN: Fuck off.

MARK: Yeah, not just a pretty face.

JOHN: What does a pub need an assistant manager for?

MARK: Yeah, yeah. It's all the same work. We just have different titles.

JOHN: I bet you've got a microwave.

MARK: What?

JOHN: I bet you've got a microwave.

MARK: Yeah.

JOHN: There you go. Not all the same, is it. I wouldn't have let one of those through the door. But everything slides under capitalism, dunnit. Anyway. Good show this afternoon.

MARK: Yeah, it was all right, wasn't it.

JOHN: Felt good doing it?

MARK: Fucking amazing actually.

JOHN: Yeah?

MARK: Really like – sure of it. Yeah. Certain. What the fuck is all this? Someone's kicked the hose over. It was probably you.

JOHN: Probably.

The boys in the pub start singing football songs.

JOHN: Listen to that. Piss heads.

MARK: Yeah.

JOHN: Your mates. You know what they say, don't you? By his friends shall you know him.

MARK: Yeah.

JOHN: Not often you get everyone you care about in the same room, is it.

MARK: No, it's cool.

JOHN: Good things, weddings. Break up the slog.

MARK: Yeah.

MARK starts sorting out the hose.

JOHN: Want a hand?

MARK: You're all right.

JOHN: Go on, we can start at different ends. It'll be like *Lady and the Tramp.*

MARK: All right.

JOHN: I'm glad you're working here though, that's good news. Bit of continuity. Nice to know they haven't just shipped in a bunch of Poles from Andover, you know?

MARK: We haven't got any Poles, no.

JOHN: Not that there'd be anything wrong with that, of course.

MARK: We've got a Slovenian girl.

JOHN: Oh yeah?

MARK: She's nice. She's gonna be an interior designer. And we've got two Filipino brothers called Joey and Ken. Well, those aren't their real names. They changed them when they came over to sound more English.

JOHN: What were their names before?

MARK: Joey's name was Irisjim.

JOHN: Yeah, the locals'd laugh at that.

MARK: Ken's funnier though. You'll like Ken's.

JOHN: Why?

MARK: His real name was Edward.

JOHN: That's brilliant.

MARK: Changed it from Edward to Ken to sound more English. They picked the new ones out of *Friends* and *Barbie.*

JOHN: Is that what passes for English culture in the Philippines?

MARK: They might have been spinning me a yarn. They're funny boys. Quicker than me anyway. They're both training as accountants. In Bournemouth.

JOHN: Oh yeah?

MARK: You've done your coils bigger than mine.

JOHN: That's all right isn't it?

MARK: Guess so. Stick it on the table.

JOHN: Don't you want it in the shed?

MARK: They'll water the grass out front in the morning.

JOHN: You water the grass?

MARK: Yeah. It looks nicer.

JOHN: But you water the fucking grass?

MARK: It needs water, dunnit.

JOHN: Things really have changed.

MARK: There's nothing wrong with watering the grass.

JOHN: No, no. I'm sure it's very neat and tidy.

MARK: Yeah.

The boys in the pub are singing pop songs.

JOHN: You were telling me about your Filipino mates.

MARK: Yeah. Well. Nothing really to say about them. They're my mates. Yeah. I've learned a bit of Filipino so I can understand what they're talking about when it's just the three of us, on shift. I wanted to know when they were swearing at me so I asked them to teach me all their swear words and they've only got one. Mangman ikao.

JOHN: What's that mean then?

MARK: Everything, basically. You're a cunt, you're a wanker, you're a fucktard, whatever. Ikao's you are. Ako's I am.

JOHN: Cool.

MARK: I know some other ones too.

JOHN: Go on then.

MARK: Pagod ako. I'm tired. Goutom ako. I'm hungry. Salamat. Thank you. Pashensa. I'm sorry. Bogi ako. I'm handsome. Maganda ikao. She's beautiful.

JOHN: Little Rosetta Stone aren't you.

MARK: I knew some other stuff but I forgot. Keeps me entertained on shift, trying to remember it all.

JOHN: I guess you can't entertain yourself by drinking while you work any more.

MARK: No, there's none of that. But we have a laugh. You've got to have a laugh, haven't you.

JOHN: No you haven't.

MARK: Oh.

JOHN: That's what kids think. Fun. That's not how it goes. I'll tell you how it goes, Mark. You've got to work and then you've got to die.

MARK: Oh.

JOHN: And you've got to get married, of course.

MARK: Yeah. That's quite fun.

JOHN: You wait and see, poor bugger.

MARK: Yeah, maybe.

JOHN: You'll be all right, I reckon. Keep off the drink. Don't forget her birthday. And enjoy tonight. You going on holiday?

MARK: Yeah. Bournemouth.

JOHN: Bournemouth?

MARK: Shit, sorry, no. Brighton.

JOHN: I was gonna fucking say. Christ, Bournemouth. That'd be a short marriage.

MARK: Right.

JOHN: How long have you been working here then?

MARK: 'Bout six months now I think.

JOHN: Yeah? It's so weird to think you're married now.

MARK: Why?

JOHN: You're a little kid.

MARK: Little married kid.

JOHN: Christ.

MARK: Yeah.

JOHN: Where you living now?

MARK: Well, that's the bad news. We're actually living in Andover.

JOHN: Fuck off.

MARK: Nothing we can afford round here.

JOHN: That's a shame, mate, I'm sorry.

MARK: It's not what we'd want, obviously. But you do what you must, don't you.

JOHN: Of course. So you live in Andover and commute out here to work?

MARK: That's it. So how are you, anyway?

JOHN: Pretty good, actually. I contacted a stockbroker I used to serve in here when I left, and he invested the money I got from my half of the pub in futures. And the portfolio's performed pretty well, and I'm actually a millionaire now.

MARK: Seriously?

JOHN: No, course not. But I'm all right. I haven't really decided what to do with the rest of my miserable life, yet, mind.

MARK: Still?

JOHN: It's only been a year.

MARK: Yeah. All the same, John. Gotta enjoy it while it lasts, haven't you.

JOHN: I've had bits and bobs of fun, don't worry. Did a bit of travelling. The mountains of Nepal.

MARK: What was that like?

JOHN: It was all right. Mountains were nice. I'm not convinced about travelling though.

MARK: No?

JOHN: I don't know why all these eighteen year olds do it. The odd nice view, but you're basically always just looking for things to do, you know?

MARK: Oh yeah?

JOHN: Yeah. Cos there's no work, and there's only so many hours a day you can spend being fascinated by how foreign everything is. Specially at my age, when your ankles swell up. Still, kids like it don't they.

MARK: They do.

JOHN: If I had a kid I'd tell him not to bother. You get more out of getting on with something, I think, that's what I wish I could do. I just can't think of anything to get on with.

MARK: That's cos you're sad, you not liking travelling.

JOHN: Yeah?

MARK: A traveller, on his journey, changes only his skies and not his self.

JOHN: Where's that from?

MARK: Can't remember. Some book I read in the loo. Someone's Facebook cover photo.

JOHN: You kept up the reading?

MARK: There isn't time really.

JOHN: Can I ask you something?

MARK: Go on.

JOHN: I always thought you'd get out of here one day. What with all your books. Bright bloke that you are. Cos there's not much here for you, is there, unless you always wanted to be an assistant manager.

MARK: Is that a question?

JOHN: Well, are you planning on doing anything, is all I meant? Have you got a plan?

MARK: I'm making one.

JOHN: Right. Yeah.

MARK: One foot in front of the other.

JOHN: Yeah. Can I ask you something else?

MARK: Don't ask me about her, John, will you?

JOHN: I just / wondered how you were about –

MARK: It's all in the past, yeah? It's all something I'm moving on from.

JOHN: Probably a good thing. Probably good to keep trucking on.

MARK: Yeah.

JOHN: And you've found someone you love.

MARK: Yeah, I have. And I married her. Cos I didn't see the point in living in the past John, in dreaming. Cos the brave thing people do is get on with it, you know? So I married her. And when I needed a job I found a job.

JOHN: And heaven knows you're miserable now.

They laugh.

JOHN: Isn't it funny how time just seems to happen to you? And you never really seem to do anything except go along with it.

MARK: Oh, there are deliberate decisions you make along the way. I took up smoking.

JOHN: Your Dad'd be proud.

MARK: Yeah.

JOHN: I stopped drinking.

MARK: Did you?

JOHN: No. But I drink much less cos I can't get it at cost any more.

MARK: I bet. Do you wanna come and see in the kitchen, everything we've cocked up since you left?

JOHN laughs.

MARK: What?

JOHN: I don't think so.

MARK: No? Fair enough.

JOHN: I had my life in there, you know? I slept in there for fifteen years. This was my life, here.

MARK: OK.

JOHN: Sorry. Nothing to do with you.

MARK: No one's very good at jokes round here any more.

JOHN: No?

MARK: I don't know how you came up with all yours.

JOHN: Joke books mate. You didn't think I was making them all up did you?

MARK: Oh. I thought you did.

JOHN: No, read joke books to keep me sane. Hm.

MARK: I'd better go back really.

JOHN: Course.

MARK: It was really good of you to come. Meant a lot to have you there.

JOHN: Wouldn't have missed it.

MARK: You wanna come in with me?

JOHN: In a minute, yeah. Everyone still comes in then do they?

MARK: Yeah. Apart from Bill Owen. You remember Bill?

JOHN: Yeah?

MARK: Dead.

JOHN: Oh yeah.

MARK: Apart from that everyone still comes in.

JOHN: I hoped they'd stay away once I left. Not seriously. Not actually. I do know it's their pub. I just hoped a bit they might want to stick it to the man.

MARK: I don't think they think of a pint as a political act.

JOHN: Fair enough.

MARK: You'll be all right, yeah, John? You'll find something you want to do soon.

JOHN: Thanks mate. Oh, I meant to ask.

MARK: Yeah?

JOHN: Liz. The organist. Have you seen her around? I wanted to talk to her.

MARK: I think she's gone actually.

JOHN: Oh.

MARK: She said she had to head home.

JOHN: Oh.

MARK: Said she wouldn't have a drink cos she didn't like drinking and driving.

JOHN: Oh. Would you know where I could look her up, by any chance?

MARK: The church'll have her number?

JOHN: Yeah. Good thought. The church. She seem all right when you last saw her?

MARK: Yeah, she was all right.

JOHN: Mm. I had it in mind to talk to her, about something. Something. But she's gone has she?

MARK: Yeah, she left after the service.

JOHN: Well. Maybe if she's happy I'll leave it at that. Hey Mark.

MARK: Yeah?

JOHN: I bet the first thing you did when you started was block up that grate. You used to hate that, didn't you.

MARK: No, the fire's still going.

JOHN: Oh yeah?

MARK: Yeah. It's like you said, that's what we're selling, really. Sweat and dogs.

JOHN: Did I say that?

MARK: Don't you remember?

JOHN: I don't remember very much sometimes Mark. I think I fucked my head.

MARK: Don't be silly mate.

JOHN: No, I do, I think I drank myself stupid. Sometimes I don't remember much.

MARK: John.

JOHN: I'm all right. I'm happy today, this is a proper happy fucking day.

MARK: You'll find things to do, John.

JOHN: Yeah.

MARK: I remember a lot of your little sayings. Think of you a lot.

JOHN: Yeah?

MARK: Bit of a mantra that, for me. Sweat and dogs. Bit of a Bible of what I'm up to. You taught me everything I know about market positioning.

JOHN: Well that's some comfort I suppose. I don't suppose you'd know who gives out the jobs round here would you?

MARK: What?

JOHN: In your chain. You know, your – well I was just thinking, they must have other pubs need running, right? You couldn't, like, ask the right person if they need an old landlord anywhere for me, could you?

MARK: I think it's all apply online now.

JOHN: Oh.

MARK: They advertise it online and you upload your CV for central office, yeah.

JOHN: Right.

MARK: I don't really –

JOHN: No, of course, stupid thought. Just. Nah, stupid.

MARK: I can give you the web address? Get it on my phone, hang on. It'll be like / www. –

JOHN: No, you're all right mate, sorry. That's not me. I'm moving on. That's not me. I'm gonna move on.

MARK: You'll be all right.

JOHN: Yeah.

The boys in the pub start singing 'Abide With Me.' JOHN and MARK listen to them.

JOHN: Fuck, I'm a miserable bastard, aren't I. Sorry mate. You got fucking married!

MARK: Yeah!

JOHN: It's amazing, isn't it? You got your life right!

MARK: Yeah. That's a nice way of. Yeah. Day I left school I came here with Lucy. And we drank a bit and we started arguing, cos she wasn't going to leave her boyfriend, she was going out with this older guy and she told me she loved me but. And I started to get upset. Cos I knew even then, I knew it wasn't gonna happen. She was never going travelling with me. And I knew in five years' time we wouldn't know each other any more. And she stood on this bench and made me get up there with her. And she pointed at the big house and the view, and she said look over there. See that? That's the world. That's where we're gonna go. We're gonna do everything. We're gonna have the most brilliant time. And when we get back to England we won't forget each other. Because we'll have shared the whole world, won't we. We're gonna live the best lives ever. We're gonna do everything we want. And I love what I have now. But I'm so glad I had that afternoon. Cos for an afternoon, I believed that. I got to believe that.

The lights go down.

END

WHILE WE'RE HERE

For Mum and Rob.

The islands feel the enclasping flow,
And then their endless bounds they know.

Matthew Arnold, *To Marguerite – Continued*

Characters

CAROL
50s, head of electoral registration for Havant
Borough Council

EDDIE
40s, originally from Portsmouth

The play is set in Carol's living room
in Havant, Hampshire.

While We're Here was first presented by Up In Arms, the Bush Theatre and Farnham Maltings on April 26th, 2017, with the following company:

Andrew French – EDDIE
Tessa Peake-Jones – CAROL

Director, Alice Hamilton
Designer, James Perkins
Lighting Designer, Sally Ferguson
Composer and Sound Designer, Dom Coyote
Costume Supervisor, Victoria Smart
Production Manager, Jasmine Sandalli
Company Stage Manager, Charlie Young
Deputy Stage Manager, Ashley Illman
Assistant Stage Manager, Beth Absalom
Producer, Sarah Wilson-White for Farnham Maltings

SCENE ONE

The sitting room of CAROL's house. CAROL and EDDIE are making up a bed on the sofa. CAROL is sorting out a sheet. EDDIE is doing the duvet. His system, inevitably, involves getting inside the duvet cover with the duvet for a bit.

EDDIE: There was this deer, this doe, came and spied on me sometimes when I was sleeping. I'd catch her, looking at the tent when I woke up, stuck my head out. She'd look at me for a minute, then run.

CAROL: Beautiful, deer. Dapply aren't they.

EDDIE: Only at certain times of year.

CAROL: Yeah, course, when they're babies. Then they get antlers.

EDDIE: Only the males.

CAROL: Yeah, course. Like cows.

EDDIE: I use to try to work out why she looked at me. Was she afraid? Did she think I could be a source of food? Or just one animal's curiosity about another, you know?

CAROL: I don't know Eddie.

EDDIE: No. That's what's beautiful isn't it. You just look in their eyes, you know? And that's all you see.

CAROL: What on earth are you doing?

EDDIE: This is how I do it.

CAROL: I don't think it's how anyone else does it.

EDDIE: Works for me. You gotta do things how you do 'em, Carol, that's what I've found. This is a good duvet, this one.

CAROL: Leanne always used to complain the house was cold.

CAROL has finished with the sheet and moves onto the pillowcases. In a moment EDDIE will have finished with the duvet; he moves onto the pillowcases too.

CAROL: Do you have a favourite animal?

EDDIE: Guess.

CAROL: Guess your favourite animal?

EDDIE: Yeah.

CAROL: I don't know. Cows.

EDDIE: No. Whose favourite animals is cows? I like otters best. I used to say, what I really want to do, I want to make a TV show called What a Lotta Otters. Isn't that the best title you ever heard? And it would pretend to be like, a documentary, me going round the world looking at the three main different types of otters. So I'd go to Ireland and look at that kind of otter, yeah? Standard otter. And you'd see otters holding hands and swimming on their back and whatever. I'd interview a fucking otter farmer or something. And then I'd go to the Arctic. And I'd tell you, to camera, the Arctic otter has ten thousand hairs per square inch of its body. Isn't that amazing? And we'd look at them for a bit. But then, two episodes in, right, the TV show would change. Its true purpose would be revealed. I'd go to Brazil to find an Amazonian otter. You know those?

CAROL: I don't think so, no.

EDDIE: They grow up to two metres long. Bigger than us. Yeah? Amazing. Absolutely – in a fight, they will fuck up a crocodile. Yeah. Best animal. And for the final show I'd just go searching. I'd just look for one and get more and more desperate, and more and more mad. And I'd be on camera going like, whoa! Whoa! People'd be scared. And then the show would end, and I'd have told you everything you need to know about Amazonian otters. To camera. While I was mad. But we wouldn't have seen one. And people would realise, that wasn't a show about otters at all. They'd talk about it afterwards, they'd say. I know. It was a show about something else.

CAROL: What would it be about?

EDDIE: Well there you go. That's the mystery, isn't it? That's the adventure.

CAROL: I don't think people would get that.

EDDIE: No?

CAROL: There we go. That's all right isn't it.

EDDIE: It's brilliant.

CAROL: I'm sorry. I don't really go in her room that much, if I'd known she'd left it in such a state.

EDDIE: Don't be silly.

CAROL: I'll sort it all out when there's time and you can be in there, but there's no point doing it tonight if you don't mind.

EDDIE: I'm just so grateful to you Carol, you're so kind.

CAROL: It's nothing. It's a pleasure.

EDDIE: Leanne must be a proper grown up now.

CAROL: Oh, yeah.

EDDIE: Where does it go right?

CAROL: Flies by, yeah.

EDDIE: Except when you get a moment like today. Then it's like there hasn't been any time ever happened at all, or you've circled back somehow. I saw you it was like you were walking up out of the past.

CAROL: Yeah, I know. So funny. I'd only gone out for a breath of fresh.

EDDIE: Yeah.

CAROL: When Leanne still lived here I used to meet her in that park Saturdays, so we could have our lunch together, so I suppose I just wandered out thinking about Leanne.

EDDIE: Oh right?

CAROL: She worked part time in the Wilko's by there, on the tills. Half the year. The other half the year she'd move to do the camps on Hayling, that's where she's moved now, which she really loves, so.

EDDIE: That's great.

CAROL: She loves it, yeah. Really happy doing that.

EDDIE: That's really great for her.

CAROL: I met you off the bus there one time, didn't I, remember?

EDDIE: Oh my God, yeah.

CAROL: And you took me into Gregg's and bought me an apple turnover to say sorry cos you were late, and you bought a packet of custard donuts for yourself and promised you'd ration them, and I knew you wouldn't.

EDDIE: Sounds like me. So you said you were still at the council?

CAROL: I've got a job in electoral registration now, yeah.

EDDIE: No way.

CAROL: Yeah.

EDDIE: What job?

CAROL: Team leader.

EDDIE: What's that mean, that good?

CAROL: It's like manager. I'm like, head of electoral registration for Havant, actually.

EDDIE: All of Havant?

CAROL: Yeah.

EDDIE: Is that as good as it sounds?

CAROL: It is quite good, yeah.

EDDIE: I thought so, I fucking knew so! You can tell from the sound of it, I could tell that was good. Well played mate, well done.

CAROL: It's more stress than anything, really.

EDDIE: How did it happen, how come you've got such a good job? I mean, I don't mean to be rude –

CAROL: I just fell into it, to be honest. Obviously I was doing the invoicing in the depot –

EDDIE: You were good at it.

CAROL: Well.

EDDIE: Worked in the bank.

CAROL: That was my career, yeah. You remember a lot, don't you?

EDDIE: I remember everything.

CAROL: Really?

EDDIE: Total recall.

CAROL: Bloody hell.

EDDIE: Just a skill I've got.

CAROL: Well.

EDDIE: I'm distracting you. You were telling me how you got your job.

CAROL: Oh yeah. Well I just, I don't know whether you remember but when we first knew each other –

EDDIE: Your husband had left you.

CAROL: Total recall. Well I was doing whatever bit extra I could find, for money, like, and someone asked me to do some canvassing.

EDDIE: To be an MP?

CAROL: What?

EDDIE: That's when you knock on doors?

CAROL: Sometimes, but this was easier. This was just that every time you have an electoral registration signup, everyone has to get a signup form through their letterbox, see? So they can take part. And in Havant, cos it's all so close together, it's not all little villages or whatever, is it, it's cheaper to pay someone to post them by hand than send them through the post. So they hire thirty-six people to post all these forms in their evenings and weekends, that's how many people you need to do the borough. And that's the sort of canvassing I did.

EDDIE: Okay.

CAROL: They give the work to council people first off, cos it's not a proper job, it's just a few evenings, they just need it done.

EDDIE: I could do it?

CAROL: Absolutely, yeah.

EDDIE: Good to know. I'd ask you probably. If I wanted that job.

CAROL: Yeah, if we had a vacancy.

EDDIE: Good to know.

CAROL: And then I was doing that, and after a while I was asked if I wanted to join the electoral registration team. It's a team of three, a sort of part-timer at the bottom, which was me, then a deputy team leader, then a team leader. And when I joined it was Wendy was team leader and Irene was deputy and I was part-time, and then I was deputy and Irene was boss, and now it's my turn being team leader and the funny thing is that it's quite three musketeers, because Wendy's actually come back to do the part-time job now the leader's me!

EDDIE: Isn't that funny!

CAROL: Well, no, I suppose it's not really, is it, but. We meet sometimes with Irene for lunch.

EDDIE: I see the irony of it. How small the world.

CAROL: How small the world indeed.

EDDIE: You mean us?

CAROL: What?

EDDIE: Bumping into each other?

CAROL: I was just repeating you.

EDDIE: Oh. Maybe I meant us then. Must have done. Cos when you said that just then, you know. I thought of us.

CAROL: That must be it then. You said you're a recycler now, that right?

EDDIE: That's sort of it.

CAROL: Not for the council though?

EDDIE: No, don't really want a proper job right now, it'd be too – I just met this bloke in a pub did some work for a scrap yard. He gives me work cash in hand if I help out, keep me ticking over. That's why I came over this way, see.

CAROL: That sounds interesting.

EDDIE: It's all right.

CAROL: Shall we have one more drink? Seeing as we're settling you in. Celebrating your arrival.

EDDIE: Yeah, why not?

CAROL: All right.

CAROL exits to get a bottle of wine. EDDIE very quickly changes out of the clothes he's wearing, into a new t shirt he pulls out of his bag, getting it on just as CAROL re-enters.

CAROL: *(Off.)* I had a good title for a story once. Like your otter title.

EDDIE: Yeah?

CAROL: 'Everything's Battered In Bournemouth.'

EDDIE: Oh yeah?

CAROL: 'Everything's Battered In Bournemouth', yeah. It'd be a telly, about a fight that breaks out in a chip shop on a stormy night in Bournemouth, in 2008, you know, while the recession's really kicking in. And the woman behind the counter's in an abusive relationship. Every type of battered you can have, in one show, all rolled in together, and you really sort of see what's happening in the country. I think it'd star Olivia Colman.

EDDIE: Yeah.

CAROL: Or Sarah Lancashire.

EDDIE: I don't know her.

CAROL: They're both good.

EDDIE: You've thought about it quite a lot, haven't you.

CAROL enters.

CAROL: I have, actually, yeah. You've changed.

EDDIE: Well, everyone changes if you know 'em long enough.

CAROL: Your clothes.

EDDIE: I know. I was doing a funny joke.

CAROL: Very quick.

EDDIE: That's what all the nice girls tell me.

CAROL: Here you go.

EDDIE: Thanks. Why Bournemouth then?

CAROL: Alliterated. You'd be good on the telly.

EDDIE: Yeah?

CAROL: Charismatic.

EDDIE: I never really watch any TV any more.

CAROL: I suppose you can't, living as you did.

EDDIE: Exactly.

CAROL: You must miss out on so much.

EDDIE: The news.

CAROL: More important things than the news, the TV, all the TV. I don't know how you cope.

EDDIE: Sometimes I have to sit out chats at work.

CAROL: I bet you do. You can watch mine now.

EDDIE: I don't think I'd like it to be honest.

CAROL: Why not?

EDDIE: I don't know. The thought of loads of people all sitting watching the same thing at once. Like babies. I dunno. I've got enough in my head.

EDDIE sits down on the sofa.

CAROL: Is it comfy?

EDDIE: It's great. Everything's great.

CAROL: Good. I'm glad. It's gonna be nice having someone else in the house again.

EDDIE: Well hopefully I won't be under your feet for too long, you know.

CAROL: Don't think about it, it's fine. You can stay for as long as you need. Leanne probably won't come home till Christmas, she's so busy with work, so I'm on my own in the house till then.

EDDIE: Well I'll stay for as long as I can if the food's that good.

CAROL: It was good, wasn't it.

EDDIE: Yeah.

CAROL: Got it off Saturday Kitchen.

EDDIE: Oh yeah?

CAROL: Great source of inspiration, Saturday Kitchen.

EDDIE: I don't know it.

CAROL: We'll watch it together, you'll love the omelette challenge.

EDDIE: I don't think we ever had dinner together, did we. Think this was our first time.

CAROL: Wasn't really that sort of friendship, was it.

EDDIE: I'd like it if it was.

CAROL: Yes. So would I.

EDDIE: Hm.

CAROL: What?

EDDIE: Wouldn't you give anything just to go back?

CAROL: What d'you mean?

EDDIE: And have it again. To the start, even just to have the last five minutes again. Isn't it sad? And lovely, but. Wouldn't you do anything?

CAROL: You mean you and me?

EDDIE: No, I just mean being young.

CAROL: I guess so, yeah. I don't know. Where were you sleeping before, exactly?

EDDIE: Over towards Emsworth.

CAROL: Oh yeah? Nice in Emsworth.

EDDIE: Yeah.

CAROL: I used to think if I moved again I'd try to move to Emsworth, because it's not really so much of a commute when you think about it, if the trade off's being somewhere nice. But the cost. And it's not like I'd go back to renting now, and maybe I wouldn't be able to afford that either, I don't know, I haven't looked, I suppose I could look online. But wouldn't it be nice to drive to work past an oyster farm, wouldn't you feel la di da? It must have been terrible out there for you though, of course you didn't care about the oysters.

EDDIE: No, no. It's all right. Layer up if it's cold. It's not a thing. I'm just in between – defensible living arrangements, that's all, it's not a tragedy. It's only till I sort my plan.

CAROL: Your plan?

EDDIE: For my future, you know? I have actually got a bit of a plan brewing about where I'll go next, you see.

CAROL: Oh right?

EDDIE: D'you wanna hear it?

CAROL: Go on then.

EDDIE: D'you think you're ready for it?

CAROL: Sod off then.

EDDIE: No, no, sorry. I'll tell you. Rewilding.

CAROL: What?

EDDIE: That's what I'm gonna do. Rewilding.

CAROL: What's that?

EDDIE: Have you not heard of it?

CAROL: I don't know.

EDDIE: Big thing.

CAROL: Isn't it when they reintroduce wolves to Scotland?

EDDIE: That's it.

CAROL: I know about that. It's shipping beavers back to England and whatever.

EDDIE: Yeah. That's, yeah. It's about restoring historic habitats. Ecosystems, innit. The balance of things. It's rewilding the countryside, ecological – you know you press edit undo on computers? It's that, for nature.

CAROL: Why do you want to do that?

EDDIE: Why?

CAROL: Yeah.

EDDIE: Because it's amazing! You know what the same kind of work did to the red kite population in Oxfordshire?

CAROL: Something good?

EDDIE: Exactly! And that's brilliant, isn't it.

CAROL: Do we want to increase the number of wolves in Scotland?

EDDIE: The question is, do we have the right to have removed them in the first place? Maybe, right, instead of making all this fucking mess, ought we to be pressing edit undo on what we've done, you know?

CAROL: Right.

EDDIE: No?

CAROL: Well you can't press edit undo on the world, can you, that's not possible.

EDDIE: It's a manner of speaking. It's about balance, that's the thing.

CAROL: So what are you actually going to do?

EDDIE: Well, there are these charities. Really doing it, you know? Mostly up north, you know, mostly Scotland. There's more room there to get stuff done.

CAROL: Where the wild things are.

EDDIE: Yeah. And it's really busy up there, you know, it's really happening. So I'm thinking I'm gonna go up there and be part of it.

CAROL: Do they have jobs going?

EDDIE: Well a lot of it, it's more like a volunteering network at first, sort of thing. But that's how all these things start. You get your foot in the door, you work a bit for free, you meet the right people, you carve something out for yourself. That's how it happens. Bish bash bosh.

CAROL: Okay.

EDDIE. Exciting right?

CAROL: Yeah.

EDDIE: It's about putting the wonder back into things.

CAROL: Rewondering!

EDDIE: Yeah, man, yeah. You get it? You're walking along, you're in Scotland, I don't know why, but you're up a hill, you see a wolf or a boar or a bear or whatever. Imagine that!

CAROL: And you think that would make people recycle more? If there were bears?

EDDIE: It seems less exciting now I'm saying it to you.

CAROL: Is this the first time you've said all this out loud?

EDDIE: I've looked into it, it's not off the top of my head.

CAROL: No, of course. But sometimes when you say things out loud, you realise –

EDDIE: That it's a shit idea?

CAROL: No, course not. Maybe just what the challenges are.

EDDIE: Yeah, maybe.

CAROL: I don't mean to be negative.

EDDIE: Well.

CAROL: Sorry.

EDDIE: 'S all right.

CAROL: It sounds like quite an isolated sort of work.

EDDIE: I wouldn't mind that.

CAROL: No?

EDDIE: I'm usually best off keeping to myself.

CAROL: Oh yeah.

EDDIE: I don't really like people, I don't think. Best song title ever: Slipknot. People equal shit.

CAROL: Oh.

EDDIE: That's always struck a chord with me, you know. I'm like Tony Adams.

CAROL: Yeah?

EDDIE: When he was manager of Portsmouth he said if it was up to him, he'd never talk to anyone. He'd walk his dogs and have his lunch, and that'd be it.

CAROL: That'd be too lonely for me.

EDDIE: Maybe. Or maybe just peaceful.

CAROL: I don't think it's very peaceful being on your own.

EDDIE: Well. You haven't got a dog.

CAROL: No. I worry what it would be like when you had to put them down.

EDDIE: Yeah. Warm day, wasn't it. For the time of year.

CAROL: Oh, yeah, it was, yeah.

EDDIE: I like it this month. Every time it comes round. If you had to imagine what the main time for getting dark was, right, in England, the normal time, I know it changes all year but if you had to pick one, that was like, the centre, and everything else was sort of, off of that, what would it be?

CAROL: What?

EDDIE: When is the weather real, and at home, and not just a version of the weather? What month is actually England?

CAROL: I don't know.

EDDIE: I think like, or what about the seasons? Which of the seasons is like, actually what England is really like?

CAROL: Well. I suppose. Autumn.

EDDIE: That's what I think. And about getting dark.

CAROL: What?

EDDIE: I think it's normal time for getting dark in October. And everything looks right in October. That's when it's like – this is England, you know?

CAROL: You're so odd, you know that?

EDDIE: Finish this off shall we?

CAROL: If you'd like to.

EDDIE: Course I'd like to, Carol.

CAROL: I shouldn't really. I've got so much work to do tomorrow, can't believe it.

EDDIE: Yeah?

CAROL: We had a computer malfunction today, data malfunction. Trying to – well it doesn't matter what we were trying to do, I can't talk about it. Makes me feel sick to think about it. And today, I get so stressed, I went into the IT department to sort things out, and there was no one there to help me, they were all on lunch or something, and I just cried. Isn't that terrible?

EDDIE: Oh, Carol.

CAROL: I know. I think I've been under stress.

EDDIE: You shouldn't be letting yourself get stressed. It's not worth it. Nothing's worth it really, is it.

CAROL: I know, I know.

EDDIE: Shall I be mother?

CAROL: You go ahead.

He pours their drinks, hands one to CAROL.

EDDIE: You all right?

CAROL: I was just thinking how strange it is we're together here really.

EDDIE: I know what you mean.

CAROL: You never know what's going to happen to you, do you.

EDDIE gets up and moves to sit on the floor.

EDDIE: I know.

CAROL: You all right?

EDDIE: I like looking at you.

CAROL: Oh.

EDDIE: It's easier to talk when you're looking at someone than when you're sitting next to them, I think. They shouldn't do that to you. It's terrible. Getting you so stressed.

CAROL: Well. Lots of people have it worse than me.

EDDIE: All the same.

CAROL: I've got a good job and I must remember to stay glad of that, even on the bad days, you know. This tastes better the more you drink it, doesn't it.

EDDIE: Yeah.

CAROL: How like life.

CAROL laughs.

EDDIE: What are you laughing at?

CAROL: Oh, sorry, it's just a joke we have in the office. Little joke. 'How like life.' We say that about things and it makes us laugh. You know. Someone says at a meeting, we've had an exceptionally low turnout at this election. And Wendy says, or I say, or whoever, 'how like life'. It's making fun, see.

EDDIE: Out of what?

CAROL: Well I don't know, really. People who are sincere. You know, all that inspirational messages – stuff. You don't have to keep calm and carry on to work here but it helps.

EDDIE: I don't have a clue what you're talking about.

CAROL: No, you wouldn't, you don't have to work in an office.

EDDIE: I'm sure it's funny though.

CAROL: Yes, thank you, I'm aware that it's not. Just makes us laugh. I get shy I think, when I'm on my own with people.

EDDIE: Or is it just me?

CAROL: I don't know. I'm not often on my own with anyone like this. Makes me feel a bit frightened.

EDDIE: Why?

CAROL: I don't know. Maybe I feel like I don't know what's going to happen. It's just not being used to things, that's all it is. Sorry, I'm talking too much. I'm feeling very tired. You know sometimes I get very very tired. I think perhaps I'm going to go to bed.

EDDIE: Are you?

CAROL: I think I'm tired enough to sleep, yeah.

EDDIE: Come on then.

EDDIE gets up.

CAROL: What?

EDDIE: Big hug.

CAROL: Big hug?

EDDIE: Come here.

CAROL: Eddie.

EDDIE: There we go. Big hug. Let's have a little dance, come on.

CAROL: You're so silly.

EDDIE: Doo be doo be doo, be doo be doo, be doo be doo.

CAROL: Eddie.

EDDIE: What? Made you smile, didn't I? And you were getting all mardy, weren't you.

CAROL: You're so silly.

EDDIE: Thank you for this, Carol. I really mean it. I'm so grateful.

CAROL: It's my pleasure, really.

EDDIE: What you smiling like that for?

CAROL: Just you. You look better than you did this afternoon, shivering there on that bench. I'm so glad to see you looking well, Eddie.

EDDIE: Thanks.

CAROL: I'm so pleased this has happened.

EDDIE: Yeah?

CAROL: I'm so pleased to have had the chance to – well, anyway.

EDDIE and CAROL look at each other, then laugh.

CAROL: It's all right though. It's all right.

EDDIE: Yeah? Make it sound sort of serious.

CAROL: Maybe it is.

EDDIE: Yeah?

CAROL: Well you might have been the most serious I ever felt about anyone. Nice to swim in this sea again, you know?

EDDIE: Yeah. It is, yeah.

CAROL: Well.

EDDIE: You okay?

CAROL: Fine. Sore back today.

EDDIE: Yeah?

CAROL: That's getting old.

EDDIE: You're not old.

CAROL: No. Thank you for noticing. I'd better –

EDDIE: Sure you're all right?

CAROL: Totally. Don't worry. Just tired.

EDDIE: Night then Carol.

CAROL: Night night.

Exit CAROL. EDDIE sits back down on the sofa and finishes his drink, then pours himself another.

SCENE TWO

The sitting room. The bedding has disappeared. EDDIE has several carrier bags of paperwork with him.

CAROL: These are your things?

EDDIE: Yeah.

CAROL: This is how you keep it all?

EDDIE: It's sort of waterproof.

CAROL: I don't really know if it is, love.

EDDIE: Isn't it?

CAROL: Well, no. They're not sealed, are they, carrier bags.

EDDIE: It's all I had, Carol.

CAROL: I understand. Let me just get my shoes off, do you mind?

EDDIE: Sorry.

CAROL starts taking off her shoes.

EDDIE: I should have said yes to a key, shouldn't I.

CAROL: Waiting out there in the rain. Will you take a key now?

EDDIE: All right. Thank you.

CAROL: Completely fine. Not very warm today, is it.

EDDIE: Not very.

CAROL: Let me just –

CAROL leans over the sofa and chucks her shoes in the direction of the door.

There we go. Right. What are we doing with all this then?

EDDIE: Well I thought maybe I'd just get rid of it all.

CAROL: Really?

EDDIE: Clean slate. Start again. Fresh start.

CAROL: You've just carted it all the way over here, you sure you want to throw it out?

EDDIE: I can't think of anything that matters to me in here.

CAROL: No? All right.

EDDIE: Maybe you'd help me go through it all though, before I chuck it away or whatever?

CAROL: Yeah, okay.

EDDIE: Just in case. Just in case I've forgotten about something important.

CAROL: What sort of thing?

EDDIE: I don't know. Something I might want to keep.

CAROL: All right. All right, let's do that then. Give me one of those.

EDDIE: Do you mind which one?

CAROL: Whatever you think's best, Eddie.

EDDIE: Just this one, maybe.

CAROL: Great. Do you want a cup of tea before we start?

EDDIE: I'm all right.

CAROL: All right. I might sit here, I think.

CAROL sits down on the sofa. EDDIE sits down on the floor.

CAROL: How do you want to go through it?

EDDIE: Maybe let's do essential paperwork, and non-essential paperwork, sort of thing.

CAROL: How do we know which is which?

EDDIE: We decide.

CAROL: Is any of this gonna be actually essential, do you think?

EDDIE: I haven't looked at it in so long, I couldn't tell you.

CAROL: Yeah. Well let's make a start and see, shall we?

She empties the bag out on the sofa and looks through it.

CAROL: This is old letters.

EDDIE: Who from?

CAROL: Might have to be you works that out, Eddie.

EDDIE: Course, sorry.

CAROL: There you go.

CAROL hands EDDIE a letter. He scrutinises it.

EDDIE: I can't read the writing. Look at that. Like a child did it.

CAROL: So we chuck that do we?

EDDIE: Why?

CAROL: If we can't even read them.

EDDIE: But if we could read them then what would they say?

CAROL: Fair point. Maybe I'll pile up letters here and we can decide about them later.

EDDIE: Yeah. Cool. Yeah.

CAROL: I'm pretty sure that most of this is bank statements.

EDDIE: Right.

CAROL: I think they're for banks in other countries, actually, look at that, funny logo. Isn't that pretty?

EDDIE: I wouldn't know how to get into that now. I don't think there's any money in it though, it's okay, I emptied everything.

CAROL: Great.

EDDIE: So let's make a deal that anything dating more than seven years ago from the bank can go in the bin.

CAROL: Seven years?

EDDIE: In case I get audited.

CAROL: I don't know whether you need to worry about having your old Nigerian bank accounts audited, Eddie, I don't know who's going to do that. If HMRC get hold of you they'll have quite enough to worry about already.

EDDIE: So we should chuck away everything from the bank?

CAROL: I think we might as well, yeah.

EDDIE: Right. Fuck. I'm sorry. I'm finding this a bit difficult, Carol.

CAROL: I can tell.

EDDIE: It actually is very hard to throw any of this away because what if no one remembers me any more one day? You know?

CAROL: It's all right, Eddie.

EDDIE: I know. Sorry. I'm being stupid. Let's do what you say.

CAROL: Yeah?

EDDIE: Everything from Nigeria or – that's Norway, I think – in the bin pile.

CAROL: All right.

EDDIE: Where shall we put the bin pile?

CAROL: What about here?

EDDIE: Yeah. Then we can both reach it.

CAROL: Exactly.

EDDIE: I'll have a look in here. See if there's other countries.

They take a bag each, and sort it, binning old bank statements. The dialogue runs over this action.

EDDIE: Maybe we can keep the letters.

CAROL: It's all right, we can keep the letters.

EDDIE: I don't wanna take up too much space.

CAROL: You won't be taking up space, it's fine.

EDDIE: I just don't want to get rid of them in case one day I remember who they came from, in case I kept them because they were important.

CAROL: Absolutely. I understand.

EDDIE stops and looks at the bin pile. It takes CAROL a moment to notice.

CAROL: What's up, love? You all right?

EDDIE: I've been alive for so long and I haven't got anything to show for it.

CAROL: You have, Eddie. You have. In your head, you've. Just not in possessions terms, that's all.

EDDIE: I used to think I didn't want to have things. I didn't want to care about things. I didn't really want to care about anything. It's only a way of getting yourself down, innit. Look at this. I haven't got anything to show for it all.

CAROL: It's okay.

EDDIE: You've got all this.

CAROL: All what?

EDDIE: I dunno. Nice house.

CAROL: Oh, you don't wanna envy people their houses.
They're a burden as much as they're anything else.

EDDIE: D'you think?

CAROL: Imagine all the time you haven't wasted worrying
about your mortgage.

EDDIE: You said you hadn't got a mortgage.

CAROL: No, but some people.

EDDIE: True.

CAROL: And they make you a target for burglaries, houses. No
one ever burgled a tent.

EDDIE: People set fire to tents.

CAROL: And people set fire to houses, we're prey to that as
well. Feral youth. There was a terrible story in the news the
other week about a man with learning difficulties, who was
actually on the register, but no one knew that at first, who
got sort of turned into a house slave by these boys. They
moved into his house and made him, I don't know, they
weren't very nice to him, they just played their Playstations
or whatever. And then when they found out he was a sex
offender they killed him.

EDDIE: Right.

CAROL: Quite horribly, but we don't need to talk about that.

EDDIE: Right.

CAROL: But the terrible thing was the live links though. You
know on the news on your computer, they have different
live links that take you through to the related stories?

EDDIE: Right.

CAROL: Well I clicked on one. And it was a court report from
a few years earlier that was really very similar, except this

time the poor man who died hadn't been a sex offender at all.

EDDIE: Even worse then.

CAROL: And then I clicked on a live link on that page, and it took me to a very similar story from a few years earlier, except this time the learning difficulties person had been a woman, and she was an American.

EDDIE: Right.

CAROL: And I started to get so panicked. Because it was all over the world, you see. You start to realise it's happening everywhere, people are doing it to each other everywhere, there are loads of stories like this. And then I read a story about a girl who got set on fire and left in a wood and I just had to shut the page I was so upset, you know?

EDDIE: I'm sorry you got so upset.

CAROL: Well.

EDDIE: They say that about Fritzl and whatever.

CAROL: What do they say?

EDDIE: There's loads of people doing what he did. We only ever hear about the thickos.

CAROL: Learning difficulties, Eddie, you don't say thickos now.

EDDIE: Sorry.

CAROL: I don't know how there could be very many men who want a woman in their basement. It would actually be very difficult, I think. Take a lot of ingenuity. You could never have anyone round.

EDDIE: I think the world's full of people who never have anyone round.

CAROL: Well. They must be very lonely.

EDDIE: Perhaps that's why they get a woman in the basement.

CAROL: Yeah, maybe there comes a point when it seems like a good idea. I don't know why we're talking about this, it's quite disturbing.

EDDIE: Sorry.

CAROL: I think it was me who started it. I talked about the learning difficulties sex offender didn't I. I knew I was going to. Sometimes I get a thing trapped in my head and it's circling and circling and I know it's going to come out some time. And I've been on my own so much, I can never tell any more how things are going to sound when I say them to another person. I do think it's a good thing, having this house.

EDDIE: Yeah?

CAROL: Something solid. I don't want to sound like I'm not grateful for what I've had. Helps you know where you are.

EDDIE: Yeah.

CAROL: This place hasn't changed since we first moved in, you know. I've had the same landscape all my life.

EDDIE: All the time you've lived here?

CAROL: All my life nearly, yeah. Mum and Dad did a bang up job when we came here, that was the last big change.

EDDIE: Did you never want to redecorate?

CAROL: No, I redecorate. Keep doing it up when it's needed. But it's more about sprucing than changing. I just keep it all looking good. And obviously Leanne helps out as well.

EDDIE: Right.

CAROL: Anyway. Two bags done.

EDDIE: Yeah.

CAROL: Made a start. That's a good bit of work isn't it.

EDDIE: I might need your help with something else as well, actually.

CAROL: Oh right?

EDDIE: I went to my GP this morning.

CAROL: Oh, okay. Have you been struggling?

EDDIE: Well, you know. It's always a struggle really.

CAROL: Yeah.

EDDIE: I came back partly cos I thought the NHS, you know.

CAROL: Of course.

EDDIE: So I've been looking for help, yeah. I feel like I need a bit of help.

CAROL: But things aren't set up for you just yet?

EDDIE: It's slow, man. You earn whatever you get from that lot, I tell you.

CAROL: What's holding things up?

EDDIE: A lot of things are difficult. It's hard to talk about, you know?

CAROL: Of course.

EDDIE: The GP I'm with, when I registered, I was getting all my post sent to a friend, right. Now she and I aren't talking. So that's sort of difficult. Cos even if there are referral letters coming, it takes a while for me to see them. Cos she won't answer my calls.

CAROL: Why don't you change your postal address to here?

EDDIE: Yeah. Maybe, yeah. Would you mind?

CAROL: Course not, if it helped. Call the GP and get it changed and then you'll be quicker getting everything sorted.

EDDIE: It's all so fiddly.

CAROL: I know.

EDDIE: Everything about it's complicated, it's all getting blood out a stone. You tell them you're ill but if you're not gonna cut yourself you're not really ill enough for them to help you.

CAROL: I know that's how it can feel.

EDDIE: No, that's what they said to me. The quickest way to get seen is if I try and kill myself. It's a shame really, cos there was an. Attempt. But that was back in Nigeria so I don't think it'd count, I don't think it'd bump me up the list if I told them, and it gave me a bad fucking head ache and I'm in a better place now, don't wanna try it again just for attention.

CAROL: An attempt?

EDDIE: Sort of hosepipe in the window sort of thing.

CAROL: Oh, no.

EDDIE: Believe me man, the headache you get off the fumes, I fucking hated it.

CAROL: That why you didn't go through with it?

EDDIE: No. I was found.

CAROL: God, Eddie.

EDDIE: Yeah. That was the other reason I left there, I guess.

CAROL: I'm so sorry.

EDDIE: I don't think it was your fault.

CAROL: No. I'm just expressing sympathy. I'm sorry that happened to you.

EDDIE: Oh, yeah.

CAROL: You don't think you'll try it again, you feel a bit better?

EDDIE: I do, yeah. I'm fine. I'm just a bit on my own, you know?

CAROL: Yeah.

EDDIE: I think I'm the only black man in Havant.

CAROL: No.

EDDIE: Not enough of us for a football team anyway.

CAROL: No.

EDDIE: Sometimes I don't feel much less foreign here than I ever have done anywhere else. But that's all right, maybe, I know where I am on my own.

CAROL: You always quite liked that feeling.

EDDIE: Yeah, you know me Carol, don't you.

CAROL: Maybe I do.

EDDIE: I've thought of you a lot, you know.

CAROL: Yeah?

EDDIE: Wondered if I'd bump into you again somehow. Can I tell you something?

CAROL: Go on.

EDDIE: Nah, I'd better not.

CAROL: What?

EDDIE: No, no, mistake, sorry. Forget it. Anyway, what I was saying. I have to fill out a form to get the counselling. I was wondering if you could help.

CAROL: Oh. Okay.

EDDIE: Just I try to think about what to say, and I get sort of emotional, and I can't keep my mind on it.

CAROL: All right. You want to do that now then?

EDDIE: We can't now.

CAROL: Okay.

EDDIE: Form got ruined in the rain. I'll go back tomorrow and pick up a new one.

CAROL: Great.

EDDIE: Thank you.

CAROL: It's completely fine, Eddie, completely.

EDDIE starts tidying away the papers.

CAROL: Always used to push help away really, didn't you.

EDDIE: All my life.

CAROL: I ever caught you looking glum I'd ask what was up and you'd tell me a joke. You always knew so many jokes. I used to be so frightened of how easy you found everything.

EDDIE: I never thought anything was, you know.

CAROL: Really?

EDDIE: Just wanted people to think I was all right. Nothing's ever been fine. I just wanted people to think I was all right so I didn't have to talk to anyone, so I could just stay out of everything.

CAROL: Yeah.

EDDIE: Trouble is that's all very nice when you're young, but look at me. I'll never last at anything normal now, will I. I don't know. Maybe there's a reason the world works like it does, and people live how they live. Maybe it's not so small to be ordinary, in the long run, when you start to get older and think about your savings. I always felt – never liked what I had, you know?

CAROL: Even though you had so much going for you.

EDDIE: I know, that wasn't the problem. I just felt so crowded here.

CAROL: By what?

EDDIE: I dunno. I can't really say. People's troubles, you know? And they get you into bother, and you never really get over anything that happens.

CAROL: Oh, that's true.

EDDIE: Yeah.

CAROL: I remember when we came back here, after Ray left. How strange it was. Because you think to yourself, we're getting back to something, we're getting on with it, we'll pick it all up again. But it's five years later, that's the thing. You're not getting back to anything, your life's been going on, it's happening, and you've done whatever with it, you have however long left. It made me very frightened, it was a frightening time.

EDDIE: Yeah.

CAROL: Sometimes I think my whole life has been a frightening time. Well. I remember the crunch of the gravel under my feet walking back up the drive, and thinking my life might be over. I might have had all of my fun. But I was wrong, it turned out. I've had a lot of good things since. And of course I have Leanne. You never know what there is coming.

EDDIE: Leanne never calls you, does she.

CAROL: Oh, yeah, she does.

EDDIE: Oh?

CAROL: She just calls at funny times.

EDDIE: Oh right.

CAROL: Calls me at work most of the time.

EDDIE: Oh yeah.

CAROL: And she's so busy as well, all she's got going on, it has to be funny times.

EDDIE: You ought to make sure you hang out with her, Carol. Cos it's all slipping past us. You want to grab it while you can. Your own little armful of life.

CAROL: Right.

EDDIE: When I was a kid and I was growing up, I didn't live with my parents. I was fostered. Did you know that?

CAROL: Yeah, you told me that before.

EDDIE: That's how I ended up in Portsmouth. Cath and Nigel Owen, those were their names, my foster parents. They didn't mean any harm, of course.

CAROL: Yeah.

EDDIE: I lived in this white house, white parents, foster brothers, sisters coming and going, till I moved out and started my life. I used to lie awake and think about my parents, my real parents, my mum and dad. That was how I learned it. You get so little of anything. And that wasn't just my mum and dad, it was everything. All gone almost before it's happened to you. Then it's back in the dark again, and racist schoolkids, and crying and lonely all the time.

CAROL: What happened to your parents?

EDDIE: My dad died, and my mum remarried, and my step dad already had a family, and there wasn't room.

CAROL: I'm sorry.

EDDIE: Yeah. Fucking hell.

CAROL: What?

EDDIE: No, no, nothing. I'm okay. Can I tell you a story?

CAROL: All right.

EDDIE: There was a ship once called the Flying Dutchman. In the old days, a sailing ship, Blackbeard, you know. And this ship was cursed. The captain of the ship was doomed to wander the ocean, and only set foot on dry land for one night every seven years. He'd done something, I don't know what he'd done. And he could only break the curse if on that one night, he got someone to fall in love with him. Not sleep with him, I mean actually fall in love. Isn't that amazing?

CAROL: Why?

EDDIE: It's about us.

CAROL: I'm not cursed, Eddie.

EDDIE: Not like that. I mean it's what it's like, isn't it. Think about it. Trying to make land. It's about us.

CAROL: Right.

EDDIE: You don't get it.

CAROL: I don't know.

EDDIE: Think about it. You might get it.

CAROL: What's the rest of the story?

EDDIE: What d'you mean?

CAROL: That's just the setup. What happens, how does it end?

EDDIE: Oh. Well. Someone falls in love with him, and he gets to go home.

SCENE THREE

CAROL has a form and a pen. EDDIE is standing, agitated.

CAROL: Has someone been here today?

EDDIE: How d'you mean?

CAROL: There's just a smell in the air, there's a perfume. Have you had someone round?

EDDIE: I got a new deodorant.

CAROL: That must be it.

EDDIE: Yeah.

CAROL: Important to smell nice.

EDDIE: Do you think I don't?

CAROL: I didn't mean that. Come on, let's do this now. What do you want to say?

EDDIE: Well. I wanna say that I don't see the point of anything. So I can't find the energy for anything. Because every time I start to do something, I remember that in a little while I'm going to be dead, and I won't exist any more. Because there isn't a heaven or a hell, I don't think, is there. I don't see how there can be. I think that's just a swizz. I wish it wasn't, I really do. Where did I get to?

CAROL: I'm not writing it down yet, I just wanna listen and get a sense of the whole thing we're gonna put in this box, you know?

EDDIE: Yeah, good idea yeah.

CAROL: So we want to say you don't see the point in anything, because you feel like whatever you do you're gonna die, is that it?

EDDIE: Yeah. No matter how much I care about anything now, I'm still gonna end up dead, so why should I care about anything? And it's worse than that. Anything I've ever cared about till now in my life has already died. Every project I ever had has failed. Every friendship I ever had has gone. I've already lived to see all the things I ever cared about end, already, and that's only like, I dunno like halfway through the road I'm meant to be walking, so how am I supposed to feel like I could put my back into anything again? If everything's already gone to shit and I've hardly even started?

CAROL: Yeah.

EDDIE: Except you're here of course. You're here, and that's not nothing. I have got that.

CAROL: Yeah. So we want to say that you don't see how to hope for anything?

EDDIE: I see no escape.

CAROL: From what?

EDDIE: Dunno. I see no escape.

CAROL: Okay.

EDDIE: I want to show someone just once how fucking vast it is, being here. Even if it looks so stupid and so small, my life, you know. If someone would only just see. I want my life to have a meaning. And it seems so obvious to me that it can't. Because it's not like that, is it. It's just one foot in front of the other till you're dead.

CAROL: Yeah.

EDDIE: So if we put that, that'll do it.

CAROL: Okay. So what if I put something like, I see no hope for anything and that's really hard because I don't know how not to hope for things, even though I know there's no point, and I don't know how to care about anything when I know I'll be dead anyway before very long, and everything I've ever done has failed and life just feels so pointless, if we say something like that?

EDDIE: Yeah. That's what I said.

CAROL: Should we put something about the background to the situation?

EDDIE: Like all the past and whatever?

CAROL: That sort of thing.

EDDIE: Yeah, yeah we should. Then they'll know it's serious. I worry they'll think that I'm making it up.

CAROL: No one will think you're making it up. What shall we say about things that have happened before then?

EDDIE: Well. We ought to say I grew up in England but I had to leave because I had a mental breakdown.

CAROL: Is that what it was?

EDDIE: What do you think it was?

CAROL: I don't know. All I knew was that you disappeared one day, you never told me you were going. I never saw you to find anything out, did I.

EDDIE: No. I couldn't. I had to get away.

CAROL: Okay.

EDDIE: I'm sorry I did that to you.

CAROL: It doesn't matter. What else shall we say?

EDDIE: Well I got out of England. And then I didn't know what to do for a while. Cos I never – you know I had this feeling I'd got lost somewhere. Like there'd been a Plan A, but I couldn't remember it. And till I worked it out, I couldn't do anything. So I was just trying to – there was nothing I wanted to do for a long time. And I started to feel like it must be because I didn't know myself, you know, I didn't know who I was. Like, there must have been a stream running somewhere, that was me, and if I could just find it I could drink it, and then I'd know what to do with my life. But I didn't know where it was. So I kind of – well I went to Nigeria, didn't I.

CAROL: Yeah.

EDDIE: I thought if I went to Nigeria maybe I'd find myself. And it was pretty easy to get work there. Lot of drilling going on. Big Chinese companies. But there aren't any Nigerians do those engineering jobs, they get the cleaning jobs, the skilled work gets shipped in. So I didn't really meet any Nigerians, I worked with Norwegians, or whatever. I ended up feeling like a foreigner, really.

CAROL: Well you were, weren't you.

EDDIE: Yeah, that was the thing, yeah. So anyway, I did some of that. And a lot of work all over like that. Or other work, or. And I ended up a lot of places. And then one day I lost a job, and I went for a walk, and I realised it had been eighteen years since I'd been in England.

CAROL: So you came home.

EDDIE: Well, Havant was never home for me.

CAROL: Course, you were Portsmouth, weren't you.

EDDIE: Yeah, so I went back to Portsmouth first. We go home, don't we. When we need to lick our wounds. I didn't want to work on rigs or whatever any more, I was feeling quite dark when I got here really, didn't want to work at all, but I had a bit of money so I lived off that, then I needed some more so I looked for work, and I ended up here.

CAROL: Okay. And then you were living in the tent.

EDDIE: No, that was only recent.

CAROL: Oh right.

EDDIE: I had this mobile library van for a bit. Cosy. I parked it in car parks. But it blew up.

CAROL: Blew up?

EDDIE: Yeah. Normal morning. I put the key in the ignition, big fire started behind me. Three fire engines.

CAROL: Really?

EDDIE: I had a gas canister in the back to do the cooking, they thought it might go. Inside, right, inside, it was all plastic moulding, you know, the interior, and after the fire it had all melted. Looked amazing. Like the waxwork zombie things in horror movies. You know, melted faces.

CAROL: Melted faces.

EDDIE: Or that Salvador Dali clock, you know?

CAROL: Right.

EDDIE: So we'll put in some of that. And then put in the tent. And say you're looking after me but it can't last for ever and I need some proper help.

CAROL: I'm not gonna kick you out Eddie, don't worry.

EDDIE: Yeah, but I can't stay here for ever. And I have heard that before, you know. No offence, but I've heard it before from people.

CAROL: What?

EDDIE: People have told me I won't have to go before now. I've always ended up back in the tent.

CAROL: I'm sorry.

EDDIE: Well. We had some fun back in the old days, didn't we?

CAROL: Yeah.

EDDIE: Good times.

CAROL: Yeah.

EDDIE: I've always had you as a happy memory, cos we had some good times. I never went wandering cos it was what I wanted. No animal ever went anywhere it didn't have to, that's what they tell you in zoos, that's why they say it's all right that they're caged up so small. I would have liked a life in one place. It never works. Always burns me. Anyone I ever trust, they go, they send me away. It's the minute it starts to feel good then it's over.

CAROL: Are you saying that because you think there's stuff going wrong between you and me?

EDDIE: No. I'm just scared.

CAROL: Why?

EDDIE: Because I'm happy here with you. And when I feel happy I know what's coming next.

CAROL: Eddie, I think someone has been here.

EDDIE: Oh?

CAROL: There's lipstick on that mug, I don't wear lipstick.

EDDIE: Checking up on me now then?

CAROL: Not really, Eddie, you just haven't done the washing up.

EDDIE: I didn't know it always had to be done straight away.

CAROL: Has someone been round then?

EDDIE: Yeah, I had a visitor, yeah.

CAROL: Okay.

EDDIE: Sorry.

CAROL: Can I ask who it was?

EDDIE: Well it was actually my ex. You know I told you about my friend I was living with?

CAROL: Yeah.

EDDIE: It was actually her.

CAROL: Did the two of you just need to have a talk, or –

EDDIE: That's it.

CAROL: You didn't want to meet in public.

EDDIE: We needed to talk a few things over.

CAROL: Right.

EDDIE: I'm sorry, I should have asked. I didn't mean to disrespect you. I have massive respect for you Carol, I'm sorry. You know what I'm like.

CAROL: I'm gonna make some tea, all right?

EDDIE: Okay.

CAROL: Will you have one?

EDDIE: Yeah, thanks.

CAROL: All right.

SCENE FOUR

Evening. CAROL is sitting on the sofa reading. Enter EDDIE.

EDDIE: All right?

CAROL: Hello.

EDDIE: Okay?

CAROL: Yeah. You all right?

EDDIE: Not really.

CAROL: You eaten?

EDDIE: Had a kebab.

CAROL: Eddie.

EDDIE: It was easy.

CAROL: Might as well slap it straight on your thighs. Have you been drinking?

EDDIE: A bit.

CAROL: I've got some news.

EDDIE: Oh yeah?

CAROL: Good news, hopefully.

EDDIE: Go on.

CAROL: Your letter came.

EDDIE: Yeah?

CAROL: So that's positive, isn't it. Good things come to those who wait.

EDDIE: Unless they gas themselves in the mean time.

CAROL: Eddie.

EDDIE: Sorry.

CAROL: Not even in jest.

EDDIE: Sorry. Where is it?

CAROL: Here you go.

EDDIE: Thanks.

EDDIE sits down with the letter as CAROL hands it to him.

EDDIE: Feel really nervous.

CAROL: You mustn't pin your hopes on it too much, of course. It's not gonna make you feel better overnight.

EDDIE: I know.

CAROL: You only get better yourself in the end, don't you, really. Let's see what it says then.

EDDIE: I sort of don't want to.

CAROL: Why not?

EDDIE: If it says no.

CAROL: If they say no then we just look at the next option. If they say no then it'll be all right.

EDDIE: They can't say no till I open it though. So I don't wanna open it.

CAROL: But you can't do that for ever.

EDDIE: I just feel on my own. I don't wanna feel worse when I open it.

CAROL: I know.

EDDIE: I know you're helping but I feel on my own.

CAROL: It's all right. I know.

EDDIE opens the letter. He takes out a leaflet and a letter. He reads.

EDDIE: Well fuck that then.

CAROL: Oh, no.

EDDIE: I don't meet the criteria.

CAROL: Do they say anything else?

EDDIE: There's a leaflet. Can you look at it? I don't wanna look at it.

He hands CAROL the leaflet and the letter.

CAROL: Are you feeling low? You may find the enclosed leaflet helpful.

EDDIE: Well that's something to look forward to, isn't it.

CAROL: Right. Cup of tea?

EDDIE: Yes please.

CAROL: Okay.

CAROL exits. EDDIE sits in silence. CAROL comes back in again.

CAROL: It'll be a minute.

EDDIE: Yeah.

CAROL: I'm really sorry they haven't offered you more, Eddie.

EDDIE: Yeah. Ah well. Sucks, but it is what it is though, innit.

CAROL: Just have to keep on, won't you.

EDDIE: Yeah.

CAROL: Are you feeling okay?

EDDIE: I don't know. Not really. I don't think I have a choice about it.

CAROL: No, I suppose you don't.

EDDIE: I suppose I have to be all right.

CAROL: Yeah.

EDDIE: All right. I'll be all right then. Let's talk about something else. How was your day?

CAROL: Oh, fine, thanks for asking.

EDDIE: Do anything fun?

CAROL: Not much. Went to work. Came home. Had some dinner. That's about it really. What about you?

EDDIE: I don't know. I don't know how to do anything now.

CAROL: It's all right.

EDDIE: I just don't know how to get out of the feeling I'm in. I don't know what I'm gonna do.

CAROL: No.

EDDIE: You might even be right about the rewilding.

CAROL: Yeah?

EDDIE: I might not have thought it through. I think I need a project though, you know?

CAROL: Everyone needs a hobby.

EDDIE: More than that, a life, we all need a life, I think. I was thinking about it. I thought I might like to be a teaching assistant. Or nursery school or something.

CAROL: Yeah?

EDDIE: I liked school. You could think someone was in charge still. And it wasn't all. And it was still all off in the future.

CAROL: Yeah.

EDDIE: Nothing's set up and waiting for us at all, actually. No one's organised anything, you have to do all of it yourself. I'd like to be back in a school again.

CAROL: That might be a good idea.

EDDIE: I don't know. Maybe I need to just stay where I am one time. It's not so terrible, dredging for scrap. It's so terrifying that you don't get what you want. What I really wish, I wish there was some kind of system where they worked out at the start of your life how much money you were going to earn, and gave it to you up front. I'd still go into work. It'd just be so much better to know that the money was there.

CAROL: Yeah, but then what if you only got a tiny bit? And then you had to live like that.

EDDIE: I spose. I think I have to probably accept that I'm not going to have some idea that's going to make me rich. I should accept that isn't going to happen. Because it would have happened by now. I was thinking what I need to do is find somewhere I want to live, and find some work I can do there. That's maybe what I'll work on next.

CAROL: Like where?

EDDIE: I dunno. Lyme Regis or something. I like Lyme Regis. Went there once for a holiday. There's a dinosaur museum, isn't there.

CAROL: Fossil museum, I think.

EDDIE: Same thing.

CAROL: So you want to move to Lyme Regis.

EDDIE: I don't know. Just, anywhere but here. I can't believe this is my one and only life, and the whole world exists, and I've spent fucking half of it in Portsmouth, you know?

CAROL: Yeah?

EDDIE: I dunno. You're born where you're born in the end, aren't you. You always liked it here.

CAROL: It's all right.

EDDIE: You must have been lonely before I got here.

CAROL: Well –

EDDIE: Did you never want to get away from this place?

CAROL: Why?

EDDIE: Don't you think you could be doing more?

CAROL: More what?

EDDIE: I don't know. I just think if you're alive in the world, and you're living in Havant, that's quite a choice you're making. You know? You can live in the Alps, Tuscany, Outer Mongolia. You're here.

CAROL: People are happy here.

EDDIE: People value different things to me. I've never been very good at understanding things that weren't me, really. That's part of my problem. So people who want. Family and security and community and routine. I don't know about them.

CAROL: You don't know about me, you mean.

EDDIE: Maybe I don't. I feel like I do though. Feel like I know something important about you. And where you're from. When I saw you in the park the other week. I don't know. It was like the whole last twenty years of my life didn't have to have vanished. Because you were still here. Sometimes it's like time isn't passing at all, up here. It was like I might be able to walk straight back into the past.

CAROL: I felt the same.

EDDIE: Did you really never fancy it? Just packing up and going somewhere else, going away from here?

CAROL: No, I'm hefted, me.

EDDIE: You what?

CAROL: It's a thing with sheep. A hefted sheep is one that
finds its way back to its home acre if you move it away.
That's me, I'm hefted, I've got my home.

EDDIE: And what a lovely home it is too.

CAROL: Well it's all right, isn't it. I did move away for a little
bit, mind. To Hayling.

EDDIE: Yeah?

CAROL: Didn't last, it was a mistake really.

EDDIE: I thought Hayling was nice.

CAROL: Oh yeah, it's lovely. Home of the holiday camp. All
started there, after the war. Some of Billy Butlin's cousins
still run the fairground, and he was from there, you know.
It's like that, that world, they all seem to intermarry, don't
they. Not inbreeding, just – family. But the last bus back
from Havant's ten to ten. Ten to five on a Sunday. And I
was always round to Mum's because she babysat, so it was
silly. Moved back after a year.

EDDIE: That's where Leanne is now though, isn't it.

CAROL: Yeah, she likes it. It's a free room, on the site, and
you're more part of it if you stay, you know?

EDDIE: Perhaps it wasn't such a bad thing you took her to
Hayling, then. Perhaps she'd thank you for it.

CAROL: I'd never really thought of that. Isn't that a nice
thought? Thank you, that's a really nice thought. I don't
think she likes it here so much.

EDDIE: No?

CAROL: Well. It's a very empty place now. And we haven't
got anywhere good to eat, what I call a voucher code

restaurant. Not like Portsmouth. You know Portsmouth's very good now.

EDDIE: Really?

CAROL: Award-winning car park.

EDDIE: That's nice. I didn't know there was a car park Oscars.

CAROL: There's all sorts of things you'd never think would exist around, aren't there.

EDDIE: Yeah.

CAROL: People set like concrete don't they. You know they say you shouldn't make faces? Or the wind'll change and it'll stick. That's how I feel, really.

EDDIE: Don't say that, Carol.

CAROL: It's just how I feel.

EDDIE: I'm sorry.

CAROL: Nothing to be done I don't think, nothing for it.

EDDIE: When did you come here, when you were a baby?

CAROL: We grew up in Leigh Park after they built it. Before it was bad, you know. We moved over here when it was starting to get all rough, my dad's job meant we could buy somewhere. Lucky, you know?

EDDIE: What did your dad do?

CAROL: He had a shop. I don't remember much about it. Hardware. Buckets. I couldn't tell you much else. He died when I was quite young, so.

EDDIE: Really?

CAROL: Yeah, when I was eight.

EDDIE: I didn't know that. Did your mum ever marry anyone else?

CAROL: Well, you know. He was her husband.

EDDIE: Yeah. I didn't know that about you.

CAROL: Yeah.

EDDIE: What's wrong Carol?

CAROL: I'm sorry. Oh, silly. It's funny how things take you by surprise. I was just thinking it's sad Mum never had anyone else. I hope she was happy, she was a long time on her own, I never think of it really.

EDDIE goes to her, holds her.

EDDIE: It's all right. You're all right.

He tries to kiss her. CAROL kisses him back. Then she stops.

CAROL: I can't do that.

EDDIE: It's all right.

CAROL: I'm sorry, will you get off me please? Get off me.

EDDIE: All right. I'm sorry. I didn't mean to do the wrong thing.

CAROL: We're just both feeling vulnerable, aren't we. We're just both feeling knocked off our feet.

EDDIE: Why don't you want to?

CAROL: I can't.

EDDIE: Why not? We're here, aren't we, we're together.

CAROL: I'm walled in. I'd like to get out but I can't, I'm sorry. I don't know how not to be frightened of someone any more.

EDDIE: Okay. I'm sorry.

CAROL: It's so frightening being alive isn't it, because you get to go on all of the rides just once. I think I've done this one. I think it's finished, I don't think I get to do it again.

That's what it feels like. People's lives get mapped out once they're far enough into them, don't they. I don't think this will come again. I'd rather not risk myself around these kinds of feelings. This is all twenty years ago for me, I can't go back, I can't do it.

EDDIE: I didn't mean to do the wrong thing.

CAROL: I know.

EDDIE: You never said that I mattered to you. Back then. I thought I was just someone you were seeing. I didn't know you wanted any more.

CAROL: Neither did I. I didn't know you were important then. That's hindsight's done that. I didn't know what my life was going to be about. I thought there might have been others. You know, people at work used to ask me whether I'd ever got over Ray. Not for a long time now, no one ever asks me about Ray any more. And I'd ask them, did you ever get over the person who broke your heart? And they never had, really. But it's funny, I think of that now, I can't believe I meant Ray. I feel like I must have meant you. I think I ought to go to bed.

EDDIE: Oh.

CAROL: I'm sorry. I think perhaps I need to go to sleep.

CAROL gets up.

I'm sorry Eddie. I'll see you in the morning.

CAROL exits. EDDIE watches after her, sitting up.

SCENE FIVE

CAROL stands alone.

CAROL: Dear Leanne. I thought I'd send you an email as I know it's late and you'll either be out or have gone to bed, and either way you won't want a call from me. But I'm thinking of you, so I thought I'd get in touch. I wanted to say don't worry about Christmas – I completely understand. It'll be really exciting for you to spend it in another country, I've never done that, I envy you. You're very lucky to have the opportunity, I think. It'll be good for me to have a change of routine as well. Perhaps I'll go to church or something, when I was young we used to go to church on Christmas morning, and that got us out of the house. I'm sorry I reacted funny when you told me. I think I've been under some stress. Life's been very busy the last couple of weeks, I've had an old friend staying and it sends everything flying when you have a house guest, doesn't it. I didn't tell you about him because he was actually staying in your room. I hope you won't be cross. Of course, I didn't use your sheets on the bed, I used the spare set. And he's gone now, anyway, so it's nothing to worry about, and I'm getting things back to normal. Hope to hear from you soon. Love you. Mum.

NIGHTFALL

For Hayden.

i.m. Margaret 'Peggy' Norris

O as I was young and easy in the mercy of his means,
Time held me green and dying
Though I sang in my chains like the sea.

Dylan Thomas, 'Fern Hill'

Characters

RYAN
A farmer, 20s

LOU
Ryan's younger sister, 20s

PETE
Underwater welder, 20s

JENNY
Ryan and Lou's mum, 50s

The action takes place in the garden of a
Hampshire farmhouse.

Nightfall premiered at the Bridge Theatre, London, on 1 May 2018, with the following cast in order of speaking:

Ophelia Lovibond – LOU
Sion Daniel Young – RYAN
Ukweli Roach – PETE
Claire Skinner – JENNY

Director, Laurie Sansom
Designer, Rae Smith
Sound Designer, Christopher Shutt
Lighting Designer, Chris Davey
Music, Gareth Williams
Video Designer, Ian William Galloway

Act One

SCENE ONE

A farm, late evening, almost dark. Night will fall across the course of the scene. An oil pipe runs across the stage, raised on struts above the ground so it stays level on its journey from Fawley up to Birmingham. There's a septic tank at the edge of the stage. PETE wears a welding mask and carries a welding iron. RYAN watches him. PETE fires his welding iron, and a light jumps into the sky. PETE goes to work on the silage tank. He's sealing in a tap he's just installed. From the other side of the stage LOU watches them, sipping on a bottle.

LOU: And there's no way anyone's ever gonna know?

RYAN: It's totally safe, Lou. Pipe like this loses gallons already. This runs for like a hundred miles, right? So you get leaks and dirt, loads of wastage. Sometimes it runs underground, and then you've got ploughing or roadworks. Then above ground there's corrosion. Or someone'll drive into it.

LOU: Or pikey lads might tap it and siphon some off.

RYAN: It's not pikey.

LOU: No, just fucking reckless. Has he got it?

PETE has lifted his visor.

RYAN: Safeways here we come!

PETE dumps his welding gear on the ground.

PETE: You got it then?

RYAN grabs a metal object to be screwed onto the pipe, and passes it to PETE.

RYAN: Oh yeah.

LOU: Oi Pete your arse is hanging out!

PETE: What?

LOU: *(Laughing at her joke.)* No don't worry.

PETE: Was my arse hanging out?

LOU: No, it was a joke. Cos you both look sort of like builders. And builders always have their arses out. Don't worry.

PETE: You know this is basically what I do for a living?

LOU: Is it? I thought you did skilled work.

PETE: This is skilled work.

LOU: Doesn't look it.

PETE: That's cos I'm doing it badly. I'll get this on.

RYAN: Woo!

PETE: Keep your tits on, work environment.

RYAN: Sorry.

PETE: This is a fucking SAS mission, remember. Special Forces shit.

RYAN: *Gears of War.*

PETE: Not *Gears of War*, for real.

LOU: X Box monkey.

RYAN: Fuck off.

PETE: It's on.

RYAN: Woo!

LOU: Getting proper dark now.

PETE: Don't worry. Wasn't in scouts for nothing. Hashtag prepared.

PETE fishes about in his pocket, takes out a head torch, puts it on and turns it on.

LOU: Is that the scout motto?

PETE: No, that's Durex.

LOU: Surprised you know that one, with your latex allergy.

PETE: My latex allergy is not a laughing matter.

LOU: Course not.

RYAN: You look proper Duke of Edinburgh.

PETE: Think that's when I bought it. Shall we do this?

RYAN: Fuck yeah!

PETE sets to piercing the pipe by turning a massive spanner that's tightening the bit of metal he's just attached.

LOU: How much is it gonna make us then?

RYAN: I dunno like, loads. Don't worry about it.

PETE: Ryan this is too hard, you have to –

RYAN: Oh right, sorry.

They work on turning the big spanner together.

RYAN: That it?

PETE: That's good. Right, and we have to –

The pipe is pierced, oil pours over them.

RYAN: Shit!

They tighten the valve

PETE: OK. Cool. We're fine. We're fucking fine.

RYAN: Let's have a goosey?

PETE: It's gander, you can't say goosey.

RYAN: You can say either.

PETE: You can't, it's gander. You stay back yeah?

LOU: If he's having a look I'm having a look.

PETE: It's dangerous.

LOU: You're a sexist pig.

PETE: No, I just mind less if he gets horrifically disfigured than if you do.

RYAN: Looking good, mate.

LOU: For the work of a sexist pig.

PETE: Right, hose on.

RYAN: Cool.

RYAN grabs the hose that's attached at one end to the septic tank.

RYAN: Fuck me, that's heavy.

PETE: Gotta use the proper gear.

RYAN: Jesus.

PETE: Tell you what, further back. You hold it there, and I'll –

RYAN: All right, yeah.

RYAN takes hold of the tubing further back.

PETE: You could help a bit maybe Lou.

LOU: Yeah?

PETE: Get that bit.

LOU goes to the middle of the hose and helps.

LOU: Just keep doing that?

PETE: Go slow, I gotta get it – yeah, that's sweet.

LOU: You know Mum'll freak when she sees it.

RYAN: Yeah, but I run the farm now. I'm in charge, she agreed that, I choose what we do. And this is a chance to give ourselves an edge, so I wanna take it. This is life, Lou. You need to take what you can get, or there will be fuck all for you. You there?

PETE: Yeah.

RYAN: This is so fucking exciting!

PETE: Stop shouting Ryan, focus.

RYAN: All right.

PETE: Have a pull on that then.

RYAN gives the hose a tug at the septic tank end.

RYAN: Sorted.

LOU: It's not gonna come out?

RYAN: All good.

PETE: All right then.

PETE opens the valve so oil can pass through the hose while the other two are talking, checks it doesn't fall off and disentangles himself from the pipe before going back round to the front of the septic tank to test his work.

RYAN: Think about how our lives might change. That's what matters. We could go back to Lanzarote if we had a bit of money. Or Beefa.

LOU: I don't think I'd go back to Lanzarote without Dad.

RYAN: It's different for you. I'm up to my neck, you're only here till you move back out. Mum and Dad had their whole lives to make this place work, and we live on fish fingers and beans. I'm done with that. My turn now.

PETE: It's done.

RYAN: Let's see?

PETE turns the tap and oil comes out. Both lads go mental.

RYAN: Woo! Thank you, mate. I need a drink I reckon.

LOU: You're both covered in shit, you know that?

PETE: We are a bit, aren't we.

RYAN: You got a change of clothes with you?

PETE: Inside.

LOU: You're not going in like that, she'll murder you.

RYAN: He can do what he wants, he's sorting us out.

PETE: Yeah, Lou. You used to be much more grateful when I sorted you out.

LOU: So inappropriate.

PETE: Fair enough.

PETE starts undressing.

LOU: Seriously?

PETE: Well if I can't go in with my gear on.

LOU: Fuck's sake.

PETE: What?

LOU: Nothing. You and all then. You're the one who shits yourself on nights out and walks it up the stairs.

RYAN starts undressing.

RYAN: That's not true.

LOU: It's literally true and you know it.

RYAN: I was getting in the shower to clean my jeans, how else was I gonna clean my jeans?

PETE: Better bin this lot.

RYAN: Yeah?

PETE: It won't come out.

They've undressed. They dump their things on the floor.

LOU: Quite a Vladimir Putin look going on.

PETE: Personal style icon. You got another cider?

LOU: Yeah.

LOU chucks PETE a cider and he opens it.

RYAN: We not going in?

PETE: In a sec. Quite like it out here like this, I feel like a wild man. Like a bear.

LOU: You should be aware you both look significantly less cool than you think you do.

RYAN: Can I have a bottle and all?

LOU hands RYAN a beer and he opens it.

RYAN: Ta. Well. This is awkward.

PETE: Why? Lou always liked me with my shirt off.

LOU: Fuck off.

RYAN: Told you.

He sips his cider.

PETE: I know what you're thinking about.

LOU: What?

PETE: You know.

LOU: No.

PETE: You know!

LOU: You're being boring.

PETE: All right. Strip poker.

RYAN: Really?

PETE: Lou used to love strip poker.

RYAN: Erm –

PETE: Which was weird, considering how bad you were at it. Used to skive off college and play it in her room, and you barely seemed to know the rules sometimes. I'd still have my blazer on and you'd be –

LOU: Well sometimes if your boyfriend's always saying how tired he is a girl has to try and get things moving for herself, you know?

RYAN: I might just leave you to it I think.

LOU: You fucking won't.

RYAN: All right. I don't even know how to play poker. Probably cos I didn't spend the whole of college fucking around playing cards.

PETE: To be fair, we didn't play a lot of cards.

RYAN: I was too busy getting an actual qualification, wasn't I.

PETE: What, swimming badges? Cycling proficiency?

LOU: Tractor driving for beginners?

RYAN: I'm not fucking thick. I know shit.

PETE: *(Sings.)* I can't read, I can't write, it doesn't really matter, cos my name's Ryan and I can drive a tractor!

RYAN: I know shit.

LOU: What?

RYAN: I dunno. D'you two know any constellations?

PETE: I'm not a fucking hippy, Ryan.

RYAN: All right.

PETE: Constellations, fuck off. I don't know my star sign and I haven't got dream catchers over my bed.

LOU: No, you've got Fraser Forster.

PETE: Still remember that then?

RYAN: Well I learned some. Orion and whatever.

PETE: Oh yeah?

RYAN: It's quite cool actually.

PETE: Oh right?

RYAN: They move around up there, that's cool.

PETE: Do they?

RYAN: Yeah.

LOU: Well they don't. They stay still, the earth rotates.

RYAN: Oh, yeah. Same thing. Main thing is that I've noticed if I leave the Fisher's Pond at eleven, Orion's right over the house when I park the car. But if I've been out clubbing or whatever, and come back in a cab, he's fucked off somewhere else. Isn't that great?

LOU: You're an idiot.

RYAN: Why?

LOU: You only chat like that when he's around, I'd forgotten you did this.

RYAN: What?

LOU: You know.

RYAN: No, what?

LOU: Shut up.

RYAN: What, Lou?

Beat.

PETE: I've got a joke.

RYAN: Go on.

PETE: This bloke was conducting this orchestra. Foreign bloke, didn't have that much English, and it turned out he wasn't much good at conducting either, all the musicians thought he was a right twat. And they were in their last rehearsal before some big gig, and everything was going to shit, you know? So this dude decided to read them the riot act. Really snap 'em together. And he called them all together and had a go, except his English fucked him over.

RYAN: Go on, what did he say?

PETE: He stood in front of them all. Shoulders back. Magisterial. And he looked down at them all, and they're looking at him like, who the fuck are you? And he said to them, you think I know fuck nothing. But I tell you now, I know fuck all! True story.

RYAN: That's quite good.

PETE: True story. I didn't mean to be a dick about all dream catchers, mate. Didn't know you were into it.

RYAN: You're all right.

PETE: Sorry. It is interesting. Just not the sort of thing you talk about inside, you know?

RYAN: Sure, yeah, sure.

PETE: But it is interesting. You can work out where north is and whatever, can't you.

RYAN: Yeah, exactly, yeah.

PETE: What other ones d'you know then?

RYAN: I only really know Orion. I know some names, the Plough and the Bear and whatever, but I've only looked at diagrams, I don't really know what they look like.

LOU: Plough and a bear, probably.

RYAN: Yeah, but can you see that up there? They all just look like stars to me.

LOU: Sound like pub names don't they.

RYAN: D'you think there's a constellation called the Dog and Duck?

RYAN and PETE laugh.

PETE: Tell you what, that might be the Fox and Hounds though.

RYAN: Yeah?

PETE: That bright one there, that's the fox. And all the other fucking stars, that's fucking millions of hounds.

They laugh.

RYAN: Yeah. All right Lou? You had enough of us?

LOU: No, just. In a stare, you know? You ever go into a stare? Like a little coma. There was this thing on the news. Someone dug up a septic tank in a field on the edge of a children's home in Ireland. This half buried septic tank, wasn't connected to anything. I don't think it was connected up. And this orphanage was run by the church, obviously, cos it dated from whenever and everything used to be run by the church. And they cracked the thing open and found the skeletons of like, two hundred children inside.

PETE: Fuck me.

LOU: I know right?

RYAN: Why are you telling us that?

LOU: Dunno. You know. The shit you find on farms.

PETE: You said it was an orphanage.

LOU: All right, the shit people do with septic tanks.

PETE: What's the difference between a bowling ball and a dead baby?

RYAN: Mate.

PETE: You used to laugh at that.

RYAN: In school. Real world now, innit, you can't do dead baby jokes.

PETE: Yeah, all right, sorry. It is a bit funny though.

LOU: It's really not.

PETE: Always liked a joke, you and me. What's funnier than a dead baby in a clown suit? Oh, wait, no, I've got that wrong.

LOU: You're disgusting.

The sound of a car parking. Lights strafe their faces.

LOU: That Mum?

RYAN: Shit.

LOU: She seen us?

RYAN: Thought she was back tomorrow?

LOU: Yeah, me too.

RYAN: Oh, fuck.

Enter JENNY.

JENNY: All right Pete.

PETE: All right Jenny. How's erm, how's things?

JENNY: What's going on here?

RYAN: Pete's been helping me sort some broken gear.

JENNY: What's that hosepipe?

RYAN: That? That's something we're mending.

JENNY: What are you doing?

RYAN: Well, it's an idea we had. What we're doing right, what we're doing is siphoning a bit of spare oil out of this pipe into this tank, so we can use it round the farm and save a bit of money.

JENNY: What?

RYAN: It's totally safe. It's just something Pete came up with to help us out a bit.

JENNY: What the hell do you think you're doing?

RYAN: What?

JENNY: How could you do that without talking to me?

RYAN: Yeah, but the thing is, you can only really tap into it safely when the pipe's closed for cleaning. So Pete checked the cleaning rotas, and it was this weekend, and you were away visiting Grandma. So we had to go ahead while we could.

JENNY: That's completely irrelevant.

RYAN: No, it had to be now.

JENNY: It didn't have to happen at all, Ryan, what were you thinking?

PETE: It's very safe though, Jenny. Cos no one ever actually checks these pipes, unless something breaks. They just run a machine through when they need to clean it, it's robots, it's not people.

JENNY: It's not so much getting caught as doing it in the first place I'm questioning, Pete, I don't understand why you've done this.

RYAN: All right Mum, chill out.

JENNY: I want you to take it out.

RYAN: Why?

JENNY: You can't leave it like that, all right? Take it apart again.

PETE: That wouldn't be very easy, though.

JENNY: Why not?

PETE: I've made a massive hole in it now.

JENNY: So close it back up again.

RYAN: Mum, think about this for a minute. I'm sorry I didn't tell you in advance. But I knew you wouldn't be OK with it.

JENNY: Got that right.

RYAN: Come on Mum, don't be like this.

JENNY: D'you know what? I can't talk to you now, Ryan. I'm too tired to have a row, I don't want to start, all right? Lou, I'm going in.

LOU: OK.

JENNY: D'you want to come in with me?

LOU: All right.

JENNY: Thank you. Let's get away from this. I'm sorry Pete, I'd like to be more welcoming, but I'm a bit shocked, you understand?

PETE: I'm sorry if I've upset you, Jenny.

JENNY: It's not – Ryan, we'll talk about this in the morning, OK? We'll talk when you've calmed down. Come on love.

JENNY exits.

LOU: I'd better go after her.

RYAN: You don't have to.

LOU: No, but I better had.

LOU exits.

RYAN: Fuck's sake.

PETE: She'll be all right.

RYAN: Pisses me off.

PETE: You knew she'd be weird about it.

RYAN: At least I'm trying things. Why would you keep doing something that doesn't work? That's the definition of – I dunno, it's the definition of something fucking stupid.

RYAN tries not to cry.

PETE: You all right mate?

RYAN: I'm fine. Fuck it anyway. I'm so fucking glad you're back.

PETE: Yeah?

RYAN: Fucking band's back together, you know? Till tonight, we were sinking. I've felt like I was drowning this last year.

PETE: We won't let you go under mate. Fuck me, what's Hampshire for if it isn't for keeping you here and making the bread that feeds us? People like you go down, you take the whole thing with you. You're the anchor, Ryan. We're the links in the chain.

RYAN: I'm the anchor?

PETE: That's it.

RYAN: Yeah. Fucking right, man.

PETE: Your mum'll be all right. Lou'll talk her round.

RYAN: You think?

PETE: She'll talk her down, she gets it.

RYAN: I dunno, man.

PETE: What?

RYAN: It's not how it was for her.

PETE: How so?

RYAN: She's checked out a little bit. First week she was in the new job, they made an offer for the land.

PETE: Yeah?

RYAN: To build twenty new houses, all along here. Mum wouldn't look at it.

PETE: Good offer?

RYAN: Good enough. She said to me, you ever change your mind, you let me know. She wants different things to me these days. Is that why you've helped, is it Lou?

PETE: I'm just trying to help you.

RYAN: Yeah?

PETE: What?

RYAN: No agenda here mate. Mum'll have her hackles up about you.

PETE: Course.

RYAN: She thinks you're the antichrist.

PETE: That's just the way I do my hair.

They laugh.

PETE: It was good to see her, obviously.

RYAN: What, Mum?

PETE: Fuck off. Lou.

RYAN: D'you still feel like you – you know.

PETE: I was wondering whether she'd wanna go for a drink some time.

RYAN: Yeah?

PETE: I dunno whether she'd be up for it though.

RYAN: We don't really talk about stuff like that.

PETE: No, course. Anyway. I've got a new job lined up.

RYAN: Serious?

PETE: Yeah.

RYAN: What?

PETE: Just oil stuff. Good gig.

RYAN: Oh, I'm so fucking glad, mate. Fuck. I'm so happy there's work for you again.

PETE: Yeah.

RYAN: I know I've said it before, but I've been so cut up, what happened. I know I didn't do my bit.

PETE: It's not like that. Don't think like that.

RYAN: But when I got off, ever since I got off. I know I was lucky. And I'm so sorry about that. And I'm so fucking glad that you can move on from it. I thought you'd never speak to me again.

PETE: Why?

RYAN: Thought I wouldn't deserve to be mates with you anymore. It was nothing to do with you, you know. When Lou stopped visiting.

PETE: I get it.

RYAN: Bag searches, and. I mean it was stressful enough for me when I went in, you know? For Lou, going in there to see her boyfriend, that's heavy, innit.

PETE: Exactly.

RYAN: It was just more than she could handle after Dad.

PETE: Right. Just as hard for her as it is for you, innit.

RYAN: Course.

PETE: And your mum and all.

RYAN: Course.

PETE: Still only yesterday really, wasn't it.

RYAN: No.

PETE: No?

RYAN: It doesn't feel like it was yesterday. It feels like it's now. It feels like we're still losing him now. Like even as we speak, someone is cutting into me. I reckon she'd go for a drink with you.

PETE: Yeah?

RYAN: Be good if she wasn't on her own all the time.

PETE: Is she?

RYAN: Well, she goes to work, obviously. But then when she's home in the evenings, that's it. Be good if she got the odd break from Bereavement Island.

PETE: It is a bit like an island.

RYAN: Desolate and hostile.

PETE: But Bear Grylls never turns up and takes you home.

RYAN: No, the cunt, he doesn't.

PETE: She hasn't been seeing anyone else then?

RYAN: No, she wanted to be on her own.

PETE: Do you ever go out?

RYAN: How d'you mean?

PETE: You're saying Lou doesn't go anywhere. Do you?

RYAN: Well, I see you.

PETE: We've had what, three drinks in the last two months?

RYAN: I don't wanna see anyone else though.

PETE: Why not?

RYAN: I know this sounds stupid. But you went away while he was still here. So you weren't here when all of it happened. When I see you, it's like I've gone back to the old time. It's like you're still back there, and I can go back there too.

With everyone else, they know what he looked like when he had to wear the wig. They know how the story ended, you're still in the good bit of the book.

PETE: Right.

RYAN: I sound mental don't I.

PETE: No.

RYAN: Maybe a drink with you, maybe Lou'd like that.

PETE: Might feel the same for her. Like it didn't happen.

RYAN: Yeah.

PETE: You should try and see other people. Gotta try and stay socialised, gotta try and get out.

RYAN: I always thought you'd end up married.

PETE: Me and Lou?

RYAN: Yeah. Stupid, I just thought that'd be what happened.

PETE: One step at a time, maybe. Would you mind?

RYAN: If you two got married?

PETE: And we were like, proper brothers?

RYAN: We've been brothers for years, mate.

PETE: Yeah?

RYAN: Course we have. That's what this is about tonight. This is the kind of shit family do for each other.

JENNY: *(Off.)* Ryan!

RYAN: I'd better go.

JENNY: *(Off.)* Ryan!

PETE: Yeah man.

RYAN: Shall I bring out your clothes? I don't reckon you wanna try going in there tonight.

PETE: No, you're all right.

JENNY: *(Off.)* Ryan!

RYAN: Speak later yeah?

PETE: Yeah, man. All right.

RYAN picks up his clothes and exits. PETE starts to get dressed again, watching the stars wheel all around him as the lights go down.

SCENE TWO

The following evening. Night will fall across the course of the scene. A patio space at the front of the farmhouse. A picnic table. There's an old metal bin on the edge of the patio. RYAN is hefting a rifle. He aims at a crow settling on a line, and shoots. He exits in the direction he fired in. JENNY enters with a pile of envelopes, a portable speaker, a string of fairy lights and a glass of wine. RYAN enters, gun in one hand, dead crow hanging from the other.

RYAN: One for the pot.

JENNY: Don't be disgusting.

RYAN: Goes to waste otherwise.

JENNY: You couldn't eat a crow.

RYAN: Why not?

JENNY sits down to open her post with a glass of wine.

JENNY: It's a criminal offence to shoot them, for one thing.

RYAN: It's not.

JENNY: It is.

RYAN: They eat the ducklings. They've had three already.

He drops the crow to the floor.

JENNY: Don't just dump it!

RYAN: Why's it a crime to shoot crows?

JENNY: It's an offence to shoot any wild birds.

RYAN: No way.

JENNY: You should know that.

RYAN: I knew it was a crime when those homeless blokes in Windsor ate swans.

JENNY: That doesn't happen does it?

RYAN: Didn't know it was all birds.

JENNY: Well. People like to say these days that everyone poor is a victim, but a thing like that reminds you.

RYAN: Thing like what?

JENNY: Let's just say I'd have to stoop very low indeed before I thought about eating a swan. I think that says a lot about a person's character.

RYAN: Well, maybe if you were hungry.

JENNY: They're a symbol of our queen.

RYAN: She might want us to eat if we were hungry.

JENNY: Oh, I can't talk about it, I get so patriotic.

RYAN: That bill's got red on it.

JENNY: Thank you Ryan, I'm not actually colourblind.

RYAN: All OK?

JENNY: Fine, don't worry.

RYAN: Doesn't have to be so scary with a bit of extra coming in. *(He gestures to the pipe.)*

JENNY: I am not spending money from that on proper bills.

RYAN: Why not?

JENNY: I'm not gonna condone it, Ryan.

RYAN: So cos it's naughty money we can only use it to buy naughty things?

JENNY: I don't want it used at all, Ryan, I want it disconnected.

RYAN: All right, just saying. If you ever wanted me to help out with the books –

JENNY: I was all right looking after them while your dad was around. I don't think they've got too much more complicated now.

RYAN: But you never did all of it. Dad was –

JENNY: This is my bit, Ryan. This is how I can contribute, you have your way you contribute. Let me have my bit.

RYAN: But we're all right, are we? We can pay that bill?

JENNY: This bill isn't Britain's most important document, it's the bloody internet or something, the phones, I don't know, it's not a big deal. Yes, I can and will pay it.

RYAN: All right.

JENNY: Everything's under control.

RYAN: All right

JENNY: Are you home now? I want to talk to you.

RYAN: Sure.

JENNY: I'm sorry I was upset last night. I shouldn't have let myself – well we don't get anywhere being emotional, do we. Nice to see Pete again.

RYAN: Yeah?

JENNY: Quite a surprise. Is he all right? Is he living at his mum's?

RYAN: Yeah.

JENNY: And what about work?

RYAN: He's got his old job back.

JENNY: Oh right?

RYAN: They've told him so, he told me last night. Took a while, but. Takes years to train a welder, doesn't it, costs a lot. So you don't just chuck 'em out because they lamp someone. They were never gonna just chuck him out. It's all tough boys down Fawley, they've had blokes go to prison before.

JENNY: I bet.

RYAN: They let him back doing contract work straight off.

JENNY: So he's been working?

RYAN: Yeah.

JENNY: And this was something he's persuaded you would be a good idea, this thing you've done, that right?

RYAN: Not really. We decided on it together.

JENNY: Right. And are you going to take it apart again?

RYAN: Why would I?

JENNY: What would your father have thought of a grubby little scam like that? He'd have nothing to do with it.

RYAN: That whole tank's full up. Think what we'll save. The heat. The light. The engines. And then if we skim any excess we can sell it. It's like a new crop.

JENNY: It's hardly a crop.

RYAN: You want a new car, don't you?

JENNY: Yes.

RYAN: So this will buy us a new car.

JENNY: Criminal proceeds though, isn't it? What's next? Brothel in the grain store?

RYAN: Brothels aren't illegal, I don't think.

JENNY: Actually they are, it's prostitution's fine, which is a complete mess, but let's not go into it. If it didn't feel so underhand I'd be fine, Ryan, I like new handbags as much as the next girl, but I want this farm to be run as your dad would have wanted, and I don't think he would have wanted that.

RYAN: Well the holes are made now, aren't they, damage is done. People would still know what we'd done, even if we took it apart again.

JENNY: Right.

RYAN: I'm sorry, but it's done.

JENNY: D'you want a glass of wine?

RYAN: I'm trying not to drink in the week, actually.

JENNY: Are you?

RYAN: Yeah.

JENNY: Really?

RYAN: Yes.

JENNY: You?

RYAN: All right.

JENNY: What's brought this on, who are you dating?

RYAN: No, it's the early mornings, that's all.

JENNY: Oh right.

RYAN: That all right with you?

JENNY: You're definitely dating.

RYAN: Mum.

JENNY: Fair enough. Just give me notice if she's coming round for dinner. And I'll need to buy some ear plugs if she's going to stay the night.

RYAN: Hilarious.

JENNY: What's going on between him and Lou?

RYAN: Speaking of noisy sex, is that the connection you just made?

JENNY: Ryan. What's the story? Have they talked? They haven't been meeting up?

RYAN: No.

JENNY: Where are they at with each other?

RYAN: I dunno.

Another crow circles towards the wire.

RYAN: Here you come, you bastard.

RYAN takes aim with the gun.

JENNY: Your father shot a Labrador here once.

RYAN: Seriously?

RYAN shoots. He misses.

RYAN: Bollocks.

JENNY: There was this old boy who'd retired down here. I think he wanted to be nearer the fishing. And he had a great fat black lab, big fat dog, I don't know what he fed it, he walked it enough, but it was enormous. And he used to walk it right across this lawn, right there.

RYAN: Joking.

JENNY: Before Dad did it up, when it was still just a scrap of field. Used it as a cut through, see, saved crossing the river. But of course it wasn't a right of way.

RYAN: No.

JENNY: So Des said to him one day, I don't know the hundredth time this bloke came trampling through, and he was having a hard day I think, your dad, or anyway he was in a foul mood, is the salient point, and he said if that dog crosses my land again I'm going to shoot it.

RYAN: Ha!

JENNY: I think it must have relieved itself against the hedge or something, but whatever the reason, he took against it. Now evidently, the gentleman who owned the dog didn't take Dad at his word. And a few days later, Dad spotted him making his way toward the field again. So he got the gun, and went up to our bedroom and settled in the window. And when the dog stepped onto the field, he got it in the neck.

RYAN: Amazing.

JENNY: Stone dead. He was a good shot.

RYAN: What did the guy do?

JENNY: Well, I don't know exactly, I wasn't there myself. But eventually I know he carried the dog off home back the way he came. Carried it in his arms, like that. Bet he regretted the weight of it then. He moved away not long after, and good riddance to bad rubbish I say, thinking the whole country's there to be walked all over by people who've come down from town.

RYAN: Amazing.

JENNY: I was cross with your dad at the time, but you do see the funny side all these years later. Are you going to get rid of that crow?

RYAN: I thought I'd string it up somewhere as a warning.

JENNY: A warning to who?

RYAN: Other crows.

JENNY: Will that work?

RYAN: It might. They're scared of scarecrows aren't they. So imagine how freaked they'll be when they circle over and see one of their dead mates hanging off the washing line.

JENNY: I don't really want dead animals hanging all round the house, Ryan. Bit *Blair Witch*.

RYAN: Suit yourself.

RYAN picks up the crow and lobs it offstage.

JENNY: Would we count that as adequate corpse disposal?

RYAN: It'll do for now, won't it? I can't be arsed burying it. Fox'll sort it out, he'll think that's delicious.

JENNY: You could put it in the bin.

RYAN: I'll do it later.

JENNY: He wants to get back with her, of course. Does he know? You know, about –

RYAN: No.

JENNY: I think she's outgrown him.

RYAN: On what evidence?

JENNY: Well, we talk every day, I do talk to her.

RYAN: What does she say makes you think that?

JENNY: It's nothing specific, it's not like that. I just have this feeling.

RYAN: Right.

JENNY sees another crow.

JENNY: Give me that.

RYAN gives her the gun. She hunches down to aim.

JENNY: I am her mother. Mothers have their intuition.

JENNY shoots. A crow falls dead onto the stage.

RYAN: Shot.

JENNY: Thank you.

JENNY goes to the crow, picks it up as RYAN speaks to her. She looks around for somewhere to put it, crosses to the bin, drops the crow in, giving RYAN the eye as she does so.

RYAN: It won't work you know, Mum.

JENNY: What?

RYAN: You can't just talk her out of whatever she's feeling. It doesn't work like that. If you go on about him you'll only piss her off, and then you're just pushing her towards him. So it won't even work, whether or not it's the right thing to do in the first place.

JENNY: I know I get too involved sometimes. It's only because I care. I know I make you angry.

RYAN: No.

JENNY: Anyone would get frustrated having to be always round their mum. God knows, it's a miracle I never killed Grandma. I'm never all right, that's the trouble.

RYAN: I know.

JENNY: It's natural to miss him. And we didn't get as long as we deserved with him, did we. You're the spit of how he looked when we first met. When I was still living at home, and he got me to move out here. He used to drive over in his car, I'd hear the radio playing while I was coming down the stairs. Sometimes I feel like I'd love to be greedy and spend a whole evening remembering him. I like to imagine if I got into bed with a pint of wine, and you and Lou sat on the bed with me, and we got out every photo anyone ever took with him in it, and laid them all out on the bed, and told each other every story we could think of with him in it till the dawn broke, or the owls were swooping, and we couldn't keep our eyes open any more, then fell asleep together you two next to me in bed like when you were little. But it never happens, a thing like that, does it.

RYAN: No.

JENNY: We're never all together somehow.

RYAN: No.

JENNY: I like to pretend he can hear me.

RYAN: Yeah?

JENNY: I like to think he's with me all the day. Even when he was alive, I used to do that. I liked things more if I imagined what he'd think of them. It was more like sharing my life.

RYAN: And you do that now?

JENNY: In my head, I talk to him about everything. In my head I'm with him now.

The sound of a car.

JENNY: That'll be Lou. Put the gun down, Ryan.

RYAN puts the gun down. Enter LOU.

LOU: Hiya.

JENNY: Hello my love. You're late back.

LOU: Am I? Sorry. I got some wine in.

JENNY: Lovely. I'll get it in the fridge shall I?

RYAN: You all right?

JENNY: Yeah. Be out in a minute.

JENNY exits.

LOU: She all right?

RYAN: We were just talking about Dad. Think she got a bit.

LOU: Oh yeah.

RYAN: Did you know he shot a Labrador out that window?

LOU: Oh, yeah. Mental.

RYAN: Did you know that story?

LOU: Dad told me. Mum kicked him out for a week after that.

RYAN: Really?

LOU: She thought he'd get us all arrested. Shouting and screaming, don't you remember?

RYAN: God. You all right?

LOU: I'm OK. Sometimes I feel really anxious when I'm coming up that drive.

RYAN: Yeah?

LOU: I dunno. Driving home sometimes, I get all jumpy like the sky's falling in.

RYAN: Well it's back in the cage again, isn't it.

JENNY enters with two more glasses of wine.

JENNY: Here's one cold already!

RYAN: Nice one Mum.

LOU: Thanks so much.

JENNY: There we go. So, darling, how are you, good day?

LOU: Yeah, all right.

JENNY: Good. Nice wine, this, isn't it.

LOU: Yeah.

JENNY: I used to be more of a chardonnay drinker but it's not so much the fashion any more. Course you won't remember

Footballer's Wives, too young. I think I'm quite influenced in my tastes by cookery programmes, you know.

LOU: Yeah?

JENNY: And what's on the shelves. God knows what I actually like best myself, I think a lot of the time I'm just cooking and drinking what people recommend on the telly. *Saturday Kitchen*'s very good for wines, I watch it on catchup sometimes when I can't sleep. Not as good now it's not James Martin. I don't know what my favourite sort of wine actually is. Do you two?

LOU: No, not really. Better white than red maybe.

JENNY: Yeah.

LOU: Is that chicken eating that crow's eyes?

RYAN: Oh, shit.

RYAN throws a stone.

JENNY: I told you to put that away.

LOU: That's dark.

RYAN: Juicy place to start. I'll just –

RYAN exits.

JENNY: Oh, I know what I wanted to do.

JENNY picks up the long string of fairy lights. She plugs them into the wall of the house and starts to string them over the stage.

LOU: They're nice.

JENNY: I thought I'd try and spruce it up, since we're spending so much time out here this summer.

LOU: Yeah, lovely. Wanna hand?

JENNY: Go on then.

LOU helps JENNY put up the fairy lights.

LOU: Where are we going with them?

JENNY: I just think sort of get 'em up in the air, you know? So you must have had Pete on your mind all day.

LOU: A bit, yeah.

JENNY: Shaken you up?

LOU: Well I was happy to see him as well.

JENNY: Yeah, sure.

LOU: Ryan tell you he might pop round tonight?

JENNY: No?

LOU: Aftercare, basically. Check there's nothing wrong with the job over there.

JENNY: Will you see him then, if he comes over?

LOU: I dunno. I don't feel like I need to hide away from him. I don't particularly feel like I need to talk to him either. Yesterday it was all right. I was scared at first, but we said hi. Then we hardly talked, they were busy. They'll be busy again tonight.

JENNY: Right. Isn't that beautiful?

LOU: Lovely.

They admire the fairy lights.

JENNY: And, check this out.

JENNY takes out her phone and fiddles with it.

LOU: Have you just discovered it's got the internet?

JENNY: No, sarky. Listen to this.

JENNY presses a button on her phone, and music starts to play from the table. Sting's 'La Belle Dame Sans Regrets'.

LOU: That's cool.

JENNY: Look.

JENNY goes to the table and picks up a set of wireless speakers.

JENNY: Weatherproof. I thought we could hang them out here, long as summer lasts.

LOU: Cool.

JENNY: Only thirty quid. Ryan'll say we should have spent it on something sensible but I thought if we're gonna save all this cash on fuel, I'll buy whatever the hell I want, so I got 'em in town this afternoon at the same time as I was getting all nice things in for tea. I never know the words to this one. Not good enough at French. What shall we listen to?

LOU: You choose.

JENNY: Well me and your dad always liked Fleetwood Mac.

LOU: All right, *Rumours* then.

JENNY: They've got other albums.

LOU: Yeah, but we're gonna listen to *Rumours*.

JENNY: Favourite song?

LOU: I dunno.

JENNY: I know what I like.

JENNY searches on her phone. 'Never Going Back Again' starts to play. JENNY dances along to it.

LOU: Such a hippy.

JENNY: You could join in.

LOU: I'm not joining in.

JENNY: Come on.

LOU: No way.

JENNY starts singing. After the first two lines, LOU joins in with the singing. JENNY keeps dancing. Before the second verse, she stops the song.

JENNY: That's enough of that.

LOU: I was enjoying that.

JENNY: Enjoying me making a fool of myself.

LOU: You were quite good.

JENNY: Silly old woman dancing, I feel all shy now.

LOU: Why, who can see us to care? Good song, innit.

JENNY: We saw them live once. Long ago.

LOU: Pete took me to see them at the O2.

JENNY: Course he did, I'd forgotten that. Well he's not all bad then, is he.

LOU: I'll do these.

LOU starts on the candles.

JENNY: Why've you got a lighter? You're not smoking?

LOU: No. They're just useful.

JENNY: Oh right.

LOU: Only a menthol after work, never killed anyone.

JENNY: I think it probably did.

LOU: I'll quit in a bit. Just a bit stressed at the moment. Work and whatever.

JENNY: They work you too hard, I think.

LOU: I'm fine. We should all stop treating each other like we're made of glass. Then maybe we wouldn't feel as fragile. I wanted to talk to you about something.

JENNY: Yes?

LOU: An idea.

JENNY: Go on.

LOU: When I move out again, I was thinking you ought to do Airbnb with my room.

JENNY: Are you thinking of moving back out?

LOU: I know last time I moved out you kept my room.

JENNY: Turned out to be good that we did.

LOU: Yeah. But I don't think you should feel you have to do that any more. When I move out next, I mean.

JENNY: Because you won't be coming home again.

LOU: I'll be making a new home.

JENNY: I don't want you to move back out.

LOU: I know. But.

JENNY: What?

LOU: We could have flown the nest a bit more than we have, I think. People are meant to go their own way, aren't they.

JENNY: That's Fleetwood Mac as well.

LOU: God it is, isn't it.

JENNY: All the time we think we're speaking for ourselves and we're only quoting lyrics. Isn't it weird? Imagine how much of our heads is made up out of other people thinking. I won't be living here for ever myself, of course.

LOU: No?

JENNY: Well. If Ryan does ever manage to lure someone back here, I guess I'd have to go.

LOU: Do you sometimes think it'd be good for you to go anyway?

JENNY: Of course not.

LOU: No, sure.

JENNY: I thought about turning the back bedroom into a granny flat, you know, Ryan's bedroom. You could build stairs up the back of the house maybe. But I haven't said anything to Ryan. I know he'd say no, and I can't really bear it. Having to go one day. And I wouldn't want to change the house, I like it how it is. I don't really know what I'm going to do if he ever meets someone.

LOU: We ought to give some thought to it all.

RYAN enters.

RYAN: Sorted. And I got the chickens in. That my glass?

LOU: Yeah.

RYAN sits down with the others on the picnic bench.

JENNY: Thought you weren't having any?

RYAN: Just a glass maybe. I hear music?

JENNY: Oh, yeah. I got some speakers.

RYAN: Cool. Put something on then.

JENNY: Oh yeah, sorry.

JENNY busies herself with her phone.

RYAN: Nice evening. That's probably Mars, look, winking at us.

LOU: Why are you shooting crows?

RYAN: Keep 'em off the ducklings.

LOU: Have the ducklings hatched?

RYAN: Yeah. Course, you haven't seen 'em, you've been out all day. They'll be asleep now. Have a look in the morning, they're cute.

Everything But The Girl's 'Amplified Heart' starts playing.

LOU: The music you like is all older than us.

JENNY: You wait and see, the world will leave you behind as well before you know it.

RYAN: We'll be in the hospice singing Eminem.

JENNY: Would you rather we listened to him?

RYAN: Don't think it's the right vibe really Mum.

JENNY: OK. Lou's been telling me she's feeling a bit funny about Pete.

LOU: Mum.

RYAN: Oh right.

JENNY: I was just saying, wasn't I, how tricky it must feel for you.

RYAN: Probably something to talk about with Pete, not us, don't you think?

JENNY: Ryan.

LOU: What do you mean?

RYAN: Just saying.

LOU: I was just chatting to Mum.

RYAN: I'm just saying.

LOU: It helps me to talk things through.

RYAN: But maybe more with Pete than Mum and me though, Lou.

LOU: I haven't talked to Pete in half a year though, have I. It's not a simple thing to start again.

JENNY: I worry about how happy he can make you.

RYAN: Mum.

JENNY: What?

LOU: Why d'you say that?

JENNY: Well you've been brought up a certain way, haven't you. And people get used to a certain way of things working. And you've been brought up into one world, all your life, and people around you, and things like that. Pete's not like that, is he. He's not close to his family. He doesn't understand our work. He does that job because it's how he can make money, he's got no feeling, not like we have a feeling for this. He's got us filling that septic tank with that muck. Because all he sees there is money, not everything else it means. I don't think he could imagine for a moment why we do what we do. And try to be a family. And look after things, so we can pass them on.

RYAN: I'd swap with him.

JENNY: No you wouldn't.

RYAN: If I got the chance. If I could have what he has, I'd take it, course I would. Modern house you can actually keep warm. Days off.

JENNY: And a year in prison and a record following him round for ever?

RYAN: That's done, that's behind him.

JENNY: You put some poor lad in a wheelchair, you can't just put it behind you. He'll be in that chair for ever.

RYAN: He fell and hit his head on a kerb. That wasn't us, not really.

JENNY: The boy you were would never have got involved. He changed you.

RYAN: Did he.

JENNY: Already had a record, that was already who he was.

RYAN: He got suspended from school, he didn't have a record.

JENNY: Adds up the same. Your Dad worked his whole life to give all this to you, how could you say you'd rather be down there? You'd just rather be away from me.

LOU: Mum, don't pick a fight, all right?

JENNY: I'm sorry. But I think that's crap, frankly, Ryan, I think you're just trying to upset me. I don't know how I'm supposed to hold us together when you talk like that. We were all right, us three. This is what happens when other people get involved. That is all of his lack of respect for anything right there, smirking at me. Flooding your Dad's farm, drowning. He comes from a different world, can you see that? He comes from a different world, and it will infect us, it'll make us sick.

RYAN: What are you talking about?

JENNY: That muck, that sludge, don't you see it?

RYAN: Why's it any dirtier what he does than me or Lou?

JENNY: Drilling for oil?

RYAN: I chuck chemicals on wheat, Mum. I chuck chemicals all round the place and I operate machinery. The idea that farming is some old pure fucking way of life is dead, if it ever even existed. I'm not a treehugger, I'm not a lentil eater, I make money, I make food. We're not druids living off roots, so don't act like you're better than him.

LOU: I don't think we were all right.

JENNY: What?

LOU: The three of us. Don't say we're all right without Pete, we're not. I did love him, Mum.

The sound of a car.

JENNY: That's him, isn't it.

LOU: Yeah.

JENNY: Oh, great.

LOU: It's all right, he's just come to check on the pipe.

Enter PETE.

PETE: Hi.

RYAN: All right mate?

PETE: Yeah, getting there. How are you Jenny?

JENNY: Fine, thank you for asking. How are you Pete?

PETE: Great. All right?

LOU: All right.

JENNY: You come to catch up about yesterday?

PETE: That's it, yeah.

JENNY: And we can catch up with you.

PETE: Yeah.

JENNY: Great. Does anyone want some wine and some nibbles maybe? I've got these cheesy things in the fridge.

PETE: Yeah. All right, thanks, yeah.

JENNY: Hang on. Let me bring a bottle out.

JENNY exits.

PETE: How is it then? I'm assuming we're OK, or you'd have called me.

RYAN: Yeah, man, it's good.

PETE: Working OK?

RYAN: I tried opening and closing the tap this morning, all good.

PETE: All right. So it sounds like we're all right then.

RYAN: It's working like a dream mate, all good.

PETE: OK. Cool.

RYAN: You wanna see it?

PETE: Yeah, erm, yeah in a bit.

RYAN: Sure, yeah, sorry.

Enter JENNY with wine and nibbles.

JENNY: Here we go then. Let's all take the weight off?

RYAN: All right?

JENNY: You sit with me, Lou.

They all sit down together.

JENNY: These are meant to be good I think.

RYAN has eaten one.

RYAN: Nice, yeah.

JENNY: Good. Want one?

LOU: Ta.

JENNY: Remember when we had that fruit salad here, Pete, and you ended up in the hospital?

PETE: Yeah.

JENNY: Your face.

PETE: Swelled right up, yeah.

JENNY: I still can't imagine what I put in there that did it.

RYAN: We thought it was probably the handle on Dad's chainsaw, wasn't it?

JENNY: Did we?

RYAN: Cos he'd left it on the kitchen table.

JENNY: Oh yeah. Anyway, your face.

PETE: You took that photo of me while I was in the hospital.

JENNY: I know. I knew we'd laugh about it later.

PETE: Yeah.

JENNY: I could go and find it if you like?

RYAN: Maybe later Mum.

JENNY: Sure, yeah. Anyway, look. I don't want to get dramatic or whatever, but I feel like I ought to say it's great to see you, Pete. I'm sure I speak for us all when I say that it's great to see you again.

PETE: Thank you.

JENNY: Because you were like a part of this family, weren't you. And that's been terrible, when we were so used to seeing you all the time, not to see you at all.

RYAN: Yeah.

JENNY: Though of course I know Ryan's been meeting up with you since you got out, I know. But you see what I mean.

PETE: Of course.

JENNY: And I don't want to get upset, but I think I should probably say, I hope I didn't come across as hostile when I saw you last night. I don't want to be hostile to you.

LOU: It's all right, Mum.

JENNY: Sorry. I just want to – it's very upsetting, something like that happening behind your back, and I do feel quite juddered by it. I won't deny that. But we ought to try to separate out the different things going on here now, you know? Because I can still be upset about that, and pleased to see you back here, can't I.

PETE: Sure.

JENNY: Good. Good. So I think that was all that I wanted to say. I don't want to make a big speech or anything. I just wanted to say, Ryan and I do need to work through the implications of what happened last night, it's not something I'm very satisfied with right now, but I don't want that to get in the way of welcoming you back onto the farm.

RYAN: Hear hear.

PETE: I really appreciate that Jenny, thank you.

JENNY: Really –

PETE: And I did want to apologise to you tonight as well.

JENNY: Oh right.

PETE: I hope you'll see all I wanted to do was help out my friend. And be a good friend. And do you a favour as well, of course. But I understand, having thought about last night, and you coming home last night like you did, I understand that it will have been a shock, and I'm sorry about that.

JENNY: Well I appreciate that.

PETE: I do think it's a good idea, what we've done, I should say that too. I do think it's smart. But of course I wouldn't have wanted to meet you again like that.

JENNY: And me, Pete. I didn't want to snap.

PETE: All right. Well I'm sorry then.

JENNY: Thank you.

PETE: These are good, aren't they.

JENNY: M and S. Get what you pay for, don't you.

RYAN: Got any more?

JENNY: I think there's another packet inside, shall I get them?

LOU: Yeah, please, Mum.

JENNY: All right. We all right for drinks?

LOU: All right.

JENNY: One sec.

JENNY exits.

LOU: I thought you two were gonna start making out in a minute.

PETE: I'm just trying to be straight with her.

LOU: Bit weird.

PETE: Well it's a weird situation, isn't it.

Music starts playing, very loudly – George Michael, 'Faith'.

PETE: Fuck me.

Enter JENNY.

JENNY: Whaddaya think of these, Pete?

PETE: Erm –

JENNY: Bluetooth speakers. Just got 'em. Cool right? I thought we could get some tunes going.

RYAN: Bit loud, Mum.

JENNY: All right, all right.

She turns the music down a bit.

JENNY: Couldn't tell the balance from inside, you know? You can operate it from your phone. Here we go, I got dips as well, and Doritos.

RYAN: Nice.

JENNY: Well then. This is nice, isn't it. This is nice.

RYAN: It's good to be able to sit outside, isn't it. Enjoy an evening.

LOU: Yeah.

JENNY: Dad loved evenings like this. All of us together, and you used to come over, and we'd all sit outside and drink.

PETE: Yeah.

JENNY: Of course that will have been the last you saw of him, won't it. After the trial, that was the last time you saw each other.

PETE: Yeah.

JENNY: Bloody hell. Isn't that amazing? All that time in between disappears, when you think of it like that.

PETE: I guess so, yeah.

JENNY: Bloody hell. I wish it would. You know we would all have liked to visit more.

PETE: I know.

RYAN: We've done this Mum.

JENNY: All right.

PETE: It's all good.

JENNY: All right.

PETE: I would have liked to have been there for you guys as well, you know. I'm sorry.

JENNY: We thought of you at the funeral. We did think of you, wished you were there.

PETE: I was there in spirit.

LOU starts to cry.

RYAN: All right mate, all right.

RYAN puts an arm around her shoulders. JENNY turns off the music.

LOU: Sorry.

RYAN: It's all right.

LOU: I'm sorry. I don't wanna cry every time, I know it's not – what a shit year though, was 2016. Fucking Prince. David Bowie. Professor Snape. Willie Wonka. George Michael. Dad.

RYAN: Yeah.

LOU: I wish no one else had died except for him.

JENNY: Why?

LOU: So people wouldn't forget about him.

JENNY: No one's going to forget your dad.

LOU: You wait. Ten years' time, people will say, 2016, that was the year all the pop stars were dying. Terry Wogan and Muhammad Ali. You wait and see. And we'll have to smile and nod and we won't know how to tell them, that didn't matter. That didn't matter at all.

JENNY: It's all right my love.

LOU: Sorry. I can't stand it. People think the most important thing in the world's some fucking referendum. Why won't anyone notice? Why won't anyone notice that doesn't matter at all?

JENNY: Yeah.

RYAN: The people who matter will always know, won't they. Our people. Us four here.

LOU: Yeah.

RYAN: And we don't need anyone else.

LOU: Maybe, yeah.

JENNY: We have to make sure that we remember him, that's all. We have to keep that much of him alive. And set the example to people, and be the example. We have to remember what it used to be like, here, when he was here, and fight to keep things as he would have wanted.

LOU: Do we?

JENNY: That'll be his legacy. All this.

LOU: Just a few fields, is that it?

JENNY: That's not what it is, love. It's more than that.

LOU: I dunno. I'm sorry, I dunno.

RYAN: You're all right.

LOU: I know.

RYAN: You don't have to be sad, then.

LOU: I'm sorry. It's just too weird, having him here.

RYAN: Oh.

LOU: I'm sorry, I can't – it's too weird to just pretend that it doesn't feel frightening you being here with us. It's making me upset.

PETE: I'm sorry.

LOU: I'm not having a go. I just can't play along, like.

PETE: Do you want me to go?

LOU: No, I just – I don't want to sit here pretending to be happy. Being civil, I don't want that.

JENNY: Lou, love.

PETE: I can go if that's easiest.

LOU: No, I don't want you to. I just don't wanna make nice with Doritos. I don't see the point in pretending the world is a nice and normal place where people have snacks, when it's not, when it's fucking evil.

JENNY: Darling.

LOU: You can't just take it away hanging up a few fairy lights, can you. It doesn't work like that.

JENNY: All right. I'm sorry.

RYAN: Maybe we ought to let you have a bit of a chat then, if you're feeling –

LOU: I don't wanna chase everyone away.

RYAN: Yeah, but maybe if you're feeling like that. Mum?

JENNY: Yeah?

RYAN: What if we go in and cook, what d'you think?

JENNY: I don't want you to feel on your own, Lou. I want you to know that you're never on your own, all right? I'm always here, I'm always with you.

LOU: Yeah. I know.

RYAN: Why don't we let you have a moment, the both of you?

LOU: Yeah, maybe.

RYAN: And you can tell Pete whatever you want to tell him.

JENNY: Ryan.

RYAN: I'm just saying. Maybe we give them a minute out here. Why don't we go in and start on the food?

JENNY: You all right if I go in?

LOU: Yeah.

JENNY: OK. You just call if you need me then, all right?

LOU: Yeah.

JENNY: You all right Pete?

PETE: I'm fine, yeah. I'm sorry, I didn't mean to –

RYAN: You're all right mate. Come on Mum.

JENNY: I'll just be inside love, all right?

LOU: All right.

JENNY: Just call if you need me.

LOU: Yeah.

    JENNY and RYAN exit.

PETE: Long time since it was just the two of us talking.

LOU: Yeah.

PETE: You all right?

LOU: No. I'm all right.

PETE: Beautiful out here. Gets good and dark. Never dark over the plant. Not so you see a sky like this one. Funny really.

LOU: What?

PETE: I spend all day drowned in steel and lights. I used to look at films of refineries in school. I'd never have guessed till I worked there all the people who keep them running come home to places like these. From a distance it looks like the moon. But when I'm working down by the water I'm watching seals bob up in the bay. And we come home and we're here, we're wild. You'd never think we lived in both worlds just from watching the documentaries. Don't you wanna talk to me?

LOU: I don't know what to say.

PETE: You don't have to say anything big, I'd just love to talk to you.

LOU: Well we are, aren't we?

PETE: Yeah. I've missed you.

LOU: Yeah.

PETE: I got too used to telling you everything. Haven't had anyone to talk to when I'm worried about stuff for too long.

LOU: Must have been hard.

PETE: It's all right. Just kept my head down. Through it all now anyway. Looking better now. I've got a new job lined up.

LOU: That's good.

PETE: They want to send me to Dubai.

LOU: Oh right.

PETE: So I'll get it all back, Lou. The things we were working towards, they're not lost. I didn't miss my chance, it's just been – on hold for a bit. And now I can get back to it. It'll be like all that never happened.

LOU: That'll be nice for you.

PETE: I'm sorry. I didn't mean to say the wrong thing.

LOU: No, you're fine.

PETE: You got a new job as well. Ryan was telling me.

LOU: Yeah.

PETE: Tell me about it then?

LOU: Well, it's just an admin job for a construction company. They build houses. We did the big new development over Fair Oak, you know?

PETE: I drive past it, yeah.

LOU: Loads of it round here now, everywhere. We buy land off of farmers, round the edge of the towns, and expand the towns out. They tried to buy this.

PETE: I heard.

LOU: Mum was spitting. I try and tell her we do good work. People need homes. We look after people really. She doesn't buy it of course.

PETE: You enjoy it?

LOU: I just wanted a reason to get out the house. First place I heard about a vacancy when I started looking. People used to be defined by their work, I think. They made that who they were. We couldn't do that now even if we wanted to, our generation. Where's the job secure enough to offer that?

PETE: Right.

LOU: And I think we know it's a swizz.

PETE: Yeah?

LOU: People used to only see their bit of the world. We can get on a plane and go somewhere. We can google anywhere. So why make your life about your work? You're alive now, aren't you. That's the only bit we know we're gonna have. I used to feel like I was waiting for something. There used to be a future. Now there isn't any more somehow, it's now instead, I'm in it. And there's nothing much to it. So I just have to do what I can to make it better. And better pretty much meant getting out the house.

PETE: Right. Ryan was saying you're not out that much though.

LOU: Did he?

PETE: Maybe I could take you out some time? If you wanted to go somewhere?

LOU: I dunno whether I can be with someone at the moment.

PETE: Weren't we happy?

LOU: Lot's changed hasn't it.

PETE: I just wondered whether you'd go for a drink with me?

LOU: I dunno.

PETE: Really?

LOU: I can't decide, I feel –

PETE: It's OK. I don't mean to put pressure on you, I'm sorry.

LOU: You're all right.

PETE: Your mum doesn't want us together again.

LOU: She thinks you're the ghost of Christmas future.

PETE: How d'you mean?

LOU: Well it so nearly happened to Ryan, going down. And obviously she thinks about that when she thinks about you.

PETE: It's not gonna happen. Des had just had his diagnosis, we were ten pints in, Ryan was mental, it was a weird night.

LOU: You know what I mean though.

PETE: Come for a drink with me one time. We could go somewhere nice, we could go to the Black Boy.

LOU: Why do we have to talk about this now?

PETE: Cos I'm going away, Lou. They'll move me so far away from here, and I don't wanna just give up on you.

LOU: Why would I spend time with you if you're going away? I'll just get hurt some more.

PETE: I never wanted to hurt you.

LOU: Why've you waited so long to come and see me?

PETE: I didn't know whether you'd want to see me.

LOU: You could have just come over.

PETE: I thought you wouldn't want that.

LOU: You could have just come.

PETE: I'm sorry. I've nearly rung you so many times. I wanted to pull my life back together first, wanted to have something to offer.

LOU: What? A move to Dubai?

PETE: Well, if you wanted it, yeah.

LOU: What the fuck would I do out there? That's not gonna happen, Pete.

PETE: A new life, new start. Isn't that the best thing could happen to you right now?

LOU: I don't need it. I don't need you going away again, I couldn't deal with it.

PETE: You wouldn't have to if you came with me.

LOU: Pete.

PETE: Nothing changed between us, did it? Why wouldn't you want to pick back up where we left off?

LOU: I was pregnant, Pete. When you went in. I didn't know, I found out later. And I lost her when Dad was ill.

PETE: Oh my God.

LOU: I miscarried.

PETE: I didn't know about this.

LOU: I didn't know how to tell you.

PETE: Oh my God.

LOU: I told Ryan not to tell you. I wanted to do it myself, you know, just didn't know how we'd ever get onto it.

PETE: I can't believe I left you on your own to go through that.

LOU: It wasn't your fault.

PETE: I can't believe I wasn't there for you. I'm so sorry.

LOU: It wasn't your fault.

PETE: We would have had a kid?

LOU: Yeah. Well, no, but –

PETE: I would have loved that.

LOU: Really?

PETE: Is that the wrong thing to say? I'm sorry, that's the wrong thing to say.

LOU: No, it's –

PETE: Please come back to me, Lou. Please don't tell me that and say I can't be there for you.

LOU: I don't know, I don't know where I'm at. I'd love us to still be together. You were the best thing ever happened to

me. But that was – I don't know whether you'd leave me
again. What would I do if that happened again?

PETE gets down on one knee.

PETE: What if I asked you to marry me?

LOU: Fuck off.

PETE: Why not?

LOU: Don't be cruel.

PETE: Let's unbreak it. Let's unbreak it. *(Sings.)* 'Whatever I
said, whatever I did, I didn't mean it, I just want you back
again, want you back, want you back, want you back for
good'. Yeah? Louise Katherine Mason, will you marry me?

LOU: You're such an idiot. You haven't got a ring.

PETE: You always said I wasn't spontaneous. We can get a ring
later. Come on.

LOU: Are you serious?

PETE: Why not? I won't leave you alone, Lou. I don't wanna
leave you alone.

LOU: Tonight is not the night.

PETE: Yeah, but it looks like it actually is though, doesn't it.

Silence.

PETE: I'll sing again.

LOU: Don't. Ask me properly.

PETE: Again?

LOU: I wanna get the feeling, I haven't had the feeling.

PETE: Shit, are you gonna say yes?

LOU: Just fucking ask me.

PETE: All right. Will you marry me?

Silence.

PETE: This is like the end of *Bake Off.*

LOU: You're such a dick. All right.

PETE: Yeah?

LOU: All right.

PETE: Fuck yes!

PETE gets up, kisses her, lifts her up.

LOU: Put me down!

PETE: You're really up for this?

LOU: Yes.

PETE: Sure you're sure?

LOU: Stop asking or I'll change my mind.

PETE puts her down. They look at each other.

LOU: Is this why you came over? This can't be what you planned to do.

PETE: No. I think I've just ended up going nuclear, haven't I.

LOU: Why is marrying me like a bombing?

PETE: It's not. I'll look after you, you know.

LOU: Yeah. I'll look after you too.

Enter RYAN.

RYAN: Erm, sorry. Did I just see what I think I just saw?

PETE: You did, yeah. I think you did.

RYAN: Oh my God.

PETE: I know right?

RYAN: Oh my God.

LOU: You all right with that bro?

RYAN: This is the fucking best thing ever.

PETE: Yeah?

RYAN: This is how it was supposed to be. We're back together. Fuck all that shit, we've come through it! We are fucking musketeers!

PETE: Yeah!

RYAN: You could move in with us.

LOU: Yeah.

RYAN: Fucking musketeers, mate, this is amazing. This is the fucking band back together!

LOU: Deep breaths Ryan.

RYAN: We gotta tell Mum.

LOU: Yeah?

RYAN: It'll be all right.

PETE: Give her a drink first maybe?

RYAN: Hang on, let me get her, Mum! Mum!

RYAN exits. PETE and LOU look at each other.

PETE: I didn't quite get in the bit about Dubai.

LOU: No, I noticed.

PETE: Gotta talk it through anyway.

LOU: Yeah, exactly.

PETE: Great. He'll be all right I reckon.

Act Two

SCENE ONE

A week later. Afternoon. Round the back of the house. RYAN is bricklaying, shirt off in the heat. PETE and LOU are watching. JENNY is idly inspecting the septic tank. By the septic tank are a pile of uncut logs and an axe stuck in one of the logs. A note – the thing about cement is that once it's mixed, it needs using, or it sets and you have to chuck it away. So RYAN will have to keep working hard through this scene.

JENNY: Do you two wanna come to *Mamma Mia* with me?

LOU: Is it at the Mayflower?

JENNY: No, London trip. Ryan doesn't want to, he's too miserable.

RYAN: It's a rip off.

JENNY: It's a joyous timeless thrilling experience and you can catch the last train home.

LOU: How much are tickets?

JENNY: You can get 'em for fifty quid I think.

LOU: Nah, you're all right.

JENNY: Don't be miserable, you can afford it.

LOU: Fifty plus trains and dinner?

RYAN: Rip off.

JENNY sings 'Mamma Mia'

JENNY: 'Mamma mia, here I go again, My my, how can I resist you?' How can you not want to experience that for real?

LOU: We've got the DVD.

JENNY: All right, forget it.

LOU: Let's see what's on at the Mayflower.

JENNY: Well you get free food poisoning thrown in there if you eat before the show, so if it's value you're looking for –

PETE: Did you get food poisoning at the Mayflower?

RYAN: No, I did. Went to Al Murray, had the prawns.

JENNY: I just thought we might like a day out in London.

LOU: Maybe.

JENNY: Now we're going to be so rich.

RYAN: You won the lottery then?

JENNY: No, but you keep telling me there's going to be so much money. Why not spend it on fun?

RYAN: I'd rather spend it on essential maintenance.

JENNY: And stupid hobbies that waste all your time.

RYAN: This is a good idea, just go with it.

JENNY: A good idea like when you thought you'd cut up all those logs last week?

RYAN: This is when you ought to cut logs. Fix the roof while the sun's shining.

JENNY: But you haven't fixed the roof, have you. You've just left an axe and a pile of bits of tree trunk in the middle of the lawn.

RYAN: I'll get it done. It's just a bit harder than it looks, that's all.

PETE: What you doing?

RYAN: Extension, innit.

PETE: Yeah?

JENNY: Making the back bedroom bigger. So we can Airbnb.

LOU: Try not to sound too excited about it.

JENNY: If it means the kitchen's bigger we can try your little schemes, as long as it doesn't take up my whole life changing sheets, you can do whatever.

PETE: This'll all be the kitchen then?

RYAN: When this is done I'm gonna knock through there, yeah. And the upstairs bedroom gets a second window, double aspect, we'll rent that out, hundred quid a week or whatever.

LOU: More light.

RYAN: Yeah.

PETE: Did you need planning permission?

RYAN: Nah, they were fine.

PETE: Really?

RYAN: Said it was OK, yeah, I called 'em up about it.

LOU: The planning office just said it was OK, over the phone, just like that?

RYAN: Yeah.

JENNY: I've only just realised that's a lie isn't it.

RYAN: No.

JENNY: You cheeky sod. I bet this does want planning permission, I bet you haven't called anyone at all.

LOU: Please don't say you've just started without telling anyone.

RYAN: It's our property, what does it matter? It's so far from the road no one's ever gonna see. Thanks mate.

PETE: Sorry.

JENNY: I can't believe you Ryan, you're so bloody slapdash.

RYAN: No, it's fine.

PETE: If you ever sold up, might have a problem, they can make you take stuff down.

RYAN: This'd be fucking brilliant if we sold up, adds value. More space. More light. More money.

LOU: But the surveyor would notice the change.

RYAN: They'd be all right about it.

JENNY: Well we're not about to sell our home I don't think, so perhaps it's not important. Maybe Ryan's right. It's our place. We'll do what we want with it.

RYAN: Thank you.

LOU: Mental.

JENNY: Englishman's home is his castle. If he wants to dig a moat then what's the problem?

LOU: Right.

RYAN: I don't think we want a moat though.

LOU: I've been making home improvements too.

JENNY: What have you done?

LOU: Replaced every door in the house with bead curtains. No, it's all right. Been having a clearout.

JENNY: Oh yeah?

LOU: Bagging up old stuff in the attic I don't need.

JENNY: I couldn't do that.

RYAN: No, that's why the house is full of rubbish.

JENNY: Memories, Ryan, not rubbish.

LOU: I've taken down all my posters. That was proper existential, that.

RYAN: You throw 'em all away?

LOU: No, they're rolled up in elastic bands. I've put them in the attic where the old stuff I don't want used to live. There's a category of thing you own, isn't there, that's stuff you don't want, but can't throw away, and just sort of keep in the garage.

RYAN: Basically describes everything you ever bought, Mum.

LOU: It'd be quite a good art exhibition. If everyone had to put the stuff they keep in cupboards on display, and be summed up by that. The things we hide and not the things we show.

JENNY: I don't know why you didn't go on with your art. You were good at it.

LOU: Not really.

JENNY: You had imagination.

LOU: I probably still have.

PETE: Me and Ryan did half your GCSE Art coursework.

LOU: Pete!

PETE: You made us do all those drawings of trees cos you said you were too busy.

JENNY: Were those not yours? I liked those.

RYAN: That was me had all the imagination then, wasn't it.

LOU: Lots of artists get other people to do the work for them. It's having the idea that counts.

PETE: I don't think you can claim that drawing a picture of a tree was your idea.

LOU: Well no, that had been done before, that's true.

JENNY: I can't believe you cheated your exams.

PETE: Nothing wrong with that if you can get away with it.

JENNY: Oh, why am I not surprised.

PETE: What?

JENNY: You find a way to bring it up again.

PETE: Excuse me?

JENNY: It doesn't matter if you get away with it, I mean really. Everything's about your scam.

PETE: I wasn't –

JENNY: The trouble is that people don't get away with it. Not for ever. I looked it up online. There were two blokes got busted three years ago in Kent. Another bloke got caught down the road from here, back in 2012. And they got three years, four years, they went to prison. You're robbing the biggest company in the entire world, they're eventually going to notice.

PETE: That's why we hid the hose. We haven't nicked enough to register, they can't see anything if they fly a drone over. If we wanted them to find out we'd have to literally call the maintenance hotline and tell them to come round, you can't tell otherwise. People get caught if they're greedy. Not if they're smart.

JENNY: The biggest company in the world. It might last for a while, but I promise you, at some point it will stop being all right. We never even wanted the pipe here in the first place. Des only let them put it through here to piss off Geoff runs the next farm.

RYAN: Really?

JENNY: Wouldn't have it at all if he didn't hate Geoff Owen so much.

LOU: He didn't hate Geoff.

JENNY: Your Dad once spent a year collecting up every stone in the west field, and piling them up in a tractor trailer. Then at midnight that New Year's Eve he drove over to Geoff Owen's top field and emptied the trailer right in the middle of it. It's a wonder they never murdered each other. That pipe was just a way of doing Geoff out of a bit of rent, I wish we'd never gone for it.

RYAN: So putting the fucking thing in was basically a scam in the first place.

JENNY: No.

RYAN: It was trying to fuck someone over.

JENNY: The money helped as well.

RYAN: And the money's helping now, that's why I done it. I don't see how it's so much worse.

JENNY: I saw Lee Hardwick here this morning, is that what he was here for, buying oil?

RYAN: He bought a few cans, yeah.

PETE: You're selling it round?

JENNY: Piccadilly bloody Circus here some days.

RYAN: Just to four or five guys. And it's fucking working, innit, the money's coming in.

JENNY: If your Dad was around he'd pull the whole thing out by the root. Someone will talk, Ryan. Someone will talk and we'll all go to prison.

RYAN: Back off a bit Mum yeah?

PETE: People know they have to be confidential though, do they?

RYAN: Yeah, course.

PETE: Cause we're all in shit if it comes out.

RYAN: It won't come out. I have to get on with this or it'll set.

LOU: We wanted to talk to you about something actually, guys.

JENNY: Oh right?

PETE: Yeah, bit of a thing. Lou and me have been talking about our work, and about where we're gonna live.

RYAN: Have you heard the same thought I did?

PETE: What?

RYAN: Well. I know I only said it was a joke the other day, right. But I've been thinking. When this is done, and the house is bigger like that. Are we completely sure that it wouldn't be fucking brilliant for you guys to live here?

PETE: Oh right.

RYAN: Fucking lager nights we'd have, you know? I've been thinking it might be an option.

PETE: Right. OK.

LOU: We were actually gonna say something else though.

RYAN: OK.

LOU: Pete?

PETE: Yeah, sure. So the thing is that I've been offered a job in Dubai.

JENNY: Dubai.

PETE: Yeah. And Lou and me have been talking about it over the last week. And we think it's something I should accept.

JENNY: Right.

PETE: So we wanted to talk to you about it, today. Cos it's got implications, obviously.

RYAN: Like what?

JENNY: You're gonna move to Dubai?

LOU: Well maybe. I know it sounds big.

JENNY: Sounds?

LOU: I'm sorry I haven't talked about it with you both till now. But the thing is, we wanted to talk through all the options first off, just me and Pete. Cos we want this to be about us, the start of our marriage. Can you see that?

JENNY: Not that you're actually married yet.

LOU: No, but you can see how this will shape a lot about our relationship, can't you. Whether I stay here or go out there with him.

JENNY: You'd be a housewife. Just sit all day in the air con.

LOU: At first, when I got over there, I wouldn't have a job. But listen. What I'm doing now isn't, like, the dream job for me. I'm not doing it because I wanted to do it for ever. And now Pete and me are a thing again, aren't we. And that gives me options I didn't know I had.

RYAN: I can't fucking believe this.

PETE: Mate, I'm sorry.

JENNY: It's traditional, Pete, that a young man comes and talks to the family of a girl before he asks her to marry him.

LOU: Mum.

JENNY: Now I can understand why that didn't happen with you two, because this engagement was very spontaneous of course, you haven't even got a ring yet –

LOU: We will.

JENNY: And in this day and age people think it's old fashioned. So of course, I didn't mind that you didn't ask me first. But I would have expected you to come to me with this.

LOU: Why should he?

JENNY: The impact this will have on our family.

LOU: I'm an adult, Mum. You don't need to be kept in the loop about everything I do.

291

JENNY: I'm not asking for everything, I'm just thinking if you're going to move to another continent, that might be worth flagging in advance.

LOU: Which is what we're doing now.

PETE: The idea is that I'd go out on my own at first. Lou would follow a bit later. If she decides that's the right thing to do. I'll need some time anyway to rent us a proper place, I'm in a hotel at first.

RYAN: I was so looking forward to all of us hanging out again.

PETE: Yeah, I know. Me too. But just to say where I'm at, my position, I kind of couldn't see how to turn this job down.

JENNY: We get that, Pete. What I don't understand is why it means Lou has to give up her career.

LOU: It's hardly a career, Mum, it's photocopying.

JENNY: You do more than photocopying.

LOU: I like the idea of going somewhere else. I think it would be interesting.

JENNY: Away from us, from here.

LOU: I've bent over backwards to be here and do my bit.

JENNY: Is that how it was? I seem to remember you needing me.

LOU: Yeah, because I did, we all did.

JENNY: Guess you just don't need me any more.

RYAN: Mum.

JENNY: So it's off to the next adventure. No thought for your family, no need to discuss it with them, just book the flight and away you go, cos that's what you and your boyfriend fancy.

PETE: But this is what we're trying to do, we're trying to discuss it with you today, Jenny. We worked out things on our side, now we've come to you.

JENNY: You're trying to pull my family apart.

PETE: What?

JENNY: That's what's happening.

LOU: Mum.

JENNY: First you turn him onto all this – guerrilla DIY. Now you wanna take her away from here.

LOU: That's so unfair.

JENNY: Is it? Why would I want you anywhere near my daughter anyway when you've done time?

PETE: I think you're forgetting what actually happened.

JENNY: I'm not.

PETE: I went to prison for something he did.

JENNY: You were both there.

PETE: He threw the punch. I was just the one got caught on CCTV. He threw the fucking punch and you know it. I went to prison as a favour to him, because of what you were going through.

JENNY: You were identified, you went to prison because you got caught.

PETE: But I could have spoken up. I could have said what happened. Got a shorter sentence. I didn't do that, out of respect for my mate, out of respect for Lou, out of respect for what you were going through. And then your husband went and persuaded his mate in the police not to bother looking for anyone else anyway, so don't go holding that sentence over me, you owe me a fucking apology for it, I ought to be thanked.

LOU: Dad did what?

PETE: You know this story better, Jenny, tell it.

JENNY: I don't remember anything about this.

PETE: Yes you do.

JENNY: It was a traumatic time.

RYAN: You know Kev Holland, knew Dad from school?

LOU: Yeah?

RYAN: Dad took him drinking. Kev said he'd wrap up the case.

PETE: What, you knew too?

RYAN: Sorry, yeah.

PETE: I thought they kept you out of it.

RYAN: I'm sorry.

LOU: Fucking hell.

RYAN: We didn't tell you Lou cos obviously for you it's complicated.

LOU: Why wasn't Dad trying to get you both off?

RYAN: You couldn't see my face on the CCTV. They had proper footage of Pete.

LOU: But he just said he didn't do it.

RYAN: That's not how I remember it.

PETE: Seriously? Don't you fucking dare mate.

A beat.

RYAN: Sorry. I'm sorry.

PETE: Fucking hell.

LOU: So it was you hit that kid?

RYAN: Yeah.

LOU: I gave up a year of my fucking life to come back here and look after you two.

JENNY: Pete was already going to prison, your dad saved who he could.

LOU: He saved family and drew the line at anyone else.

JENNY: They had him on the camera.

LOU: A fucking year I looked after you.

JENNY: How would we have told you? What would you have wanted us to say? What difference would it have made anyway?

RYAN: Pete...

PETE: I wish you'd told me you knew.

RYAN: I'm sorry.

PETE: You should have been up front about it. I might have understood if you were up front.

RYAN: You can understand now though, can't you?

PETE: I dunno. I wish you'd said.

RYAN: What was I supposed to do, Pete? Call up the station and hand myself in?

PETE: I thought I was protecting you. That was what your dad said, that was the deal. But you already knew.

RYAN: Mate, I'm sorry.

JENNY: Right. I want you to get off my land now, thank you.

PETE: What?

JENNY: I think you can go now, I want to talk to my children.

RYAN: Mum, don't be ridiculous.

JENNY: Can you get in your car and fuck off please? Do you think you could manage that for me?

PETE: All right, fine. Call me when you get out of here yeah?

LOU: Sure.

JENNY: Why does she need to get out of here?

PETE: Can I just say, before I go, and I'll go if you want, but I think you're making a joke of yourself. I think you're lying to yourself. If you think this place was all fine and I've fucked it, you're deluded. Your kids are so unhappy. You can't see that. But I care about them, so I can.

JENNY: Don't tell me I don't care about my kids.

PETE: You care about yourself, they're lifestyle appendages. All of this is just outfits you've collected to wear. I've always tried to be nice to you, Jenny, but you're being ridiculous.

JENNY: Of course, I'm ridiculous. And you're the one who's in the right. That's what children always think.

PETE: You should try and wake yourself up because your kids are gonna have to get away from this toxic fucking place if you don't change it. I've said my bit. Call me later.

PETE exits.

LOU: How could you let him sit in prison all that time?

RYAN: I didn't get any say. You know what Dad was like. When he'd made his mind up.

LOU: I stopped visiting. I can't believe it. You put someone in a wheelchair.

RYAN: I was off my nut. I'd been drinking all day.

LOU: So you hit someone.

RYAN: I'm not fucking proud of it all right?

JENNY: Ryan had much more to lose, you have to see the big picture Lou.

LOU: What?

JENNY: Des needed Ryan to be around to take over the farm. This is his life. If Ryan hadn't been around, what would have happened to it?

LOU: Ryan didn't even want the fucking farm.

RYAN: That's not true.

LOU: Neither of us wanted anything to do with all this shit. This is just the place where Dad died, this isn't our lives. Ryan didn't fucking want it.

JENNY: Maybe when you were first getting to grips with what you were taking over, maybe you did feel quite daunted by that. But I think Ryan has the maturity to recognise that there are things bigger than him that he needs to take responsibility for. This family will go on after he's gone, this is bigger than him.

LOU: That's bullshit. It's his life. You don't like it here. Tell her.

RYAN: Lou.

LOU: How could you want that for him? Look at him. How could you want him to feel like that?

JENNY: I don't know what you're talking about. I think we all spend a lot of time dancing round the jealousy you feel for your brother –

LOU: Excuse me?

JENNY: We all spend a lot of time putting up with your moods, your negativity about this place, which I think we all know springs really from you feeling hurt that it's not you who's in charge of it.

LOU: I'd have run a mile Mum.

JENNY: I wish you saw it clearer. Because you're not disinherited, you're so not, but the way you act all the time –

RYAN: I don't think that's fair at all.

JENNY: Really?

RYAN: I think Lou's done everything to help me get to grips with all the shit that comes with being here.

JENNY: Can you both stop telling me my life was shit?

Silence.

LOU: What?

JENNY: I'm sorry you don't like it. I'm sorry it's hard. I'm sorry if it's not what you dreamed of, what you wanted. But that, actually, is what life is like. That's one of the lessons you learn by growing up. Some of life is shit, and some of it you'll have to work hard at, and some of it won't be rewarding. I'm sorry that's come as a shock to you. Clearly we didn't teach you enough about that. But I think it's worth doing the hard bits because sticking at them is how you push through to the bits of life that matter. Like this place. This matters. Because it's the place where our whole lives have happened, all three of us. I can see myself, nineteen years old, hiding behind that tree, twenty-four years old, filling a basket with those apples. I can see you cutting your thumb on that pampas grass. I can see you following me out to the peg line, when you were barely walking. Our whole lives are here, and I'm sorry you have to get up early in the mornings, but that's part of the price you pay for holding onto all this.

RYAN: No one's saying it's not good us being here.

JENNY: That's all you ever say to me, you two. Everything you do I see it. You think you're miserable. You think you're cursed. You can't see how wonderful some of this is.

RYAN: We've all got a lot to get over, I don't think you can expect us to be skipping and jumping.

JENNY: No. But I don't see why you have to spend your whole time trying to twist the knife and make me feel guilty for having given birth to you.

LOU: That's mental. You should see someone, that's mental.

JENNY: Is it.

LOU: Seriously Mum, if you think that, you ought to get help.

JENNY: Don't go with him.

LOU: How could I stay after what I've just heard? You both lied to me for so long.

JENNY: But is this something you actually want?

LOU: I dunno.

JENNY: Well then.

LOU: I sometimes feel like I'm getting the bends. One minute I was just a kid in college. Then you're not allowed to be that any more. So they tell you you need money, so you find yourself a job. And all of a sudden your ambitions reduce down to that little world, and you find yourself chasing your Christmas bonus, chasing a rise, and you don't think about all the things you thought that you were gonna do when you were younger. You don't have a dream so you just go after money, cos at least that's something you can count. At least maybe you'll buy a house with it, or something like that, and that might count for something when they add you up. And suddenly you're twenty-eight and where's that gone, what happened to that? I'm going too fast through it and I'm getting crushed. I never had time to think about how to be happy. I never had time to work out whether I wanted the things that were happening to me, they happen so quickly, then they're gone. I don't want this feeling any more. I just want to feel like I'm choosing what happens to me.

JENNY: You don't sound to me like you're happy with him at all.

LOU: I'm not happy with anything, Mum. Everything I've got fucking sucks. But if I can change parts of it, I'll try that. And maybe that will make things better. So that's what I'm going to do, I'm going to try changing.

JENNY: And marry the kind of guy who takes you ring shopping in H.Samuel?

LOU: We weren't gonna buy the ring there. We were just coming up with ideas.

RYAN: I'm gonna be so gutted when you go.

LOU: You don't have to stay, you know. You could leave here.

RYAN: Yeah –

LOU: You don't actually owe anyone anything, Ryan. Not Dad, not Mum. And the world has other places in it.

RYAN: All right.

JENNY: Sometimes you're just as jealous of your sister as she is of you, I think.

RYAN: What am I jealous of?

JENNY: Well. She's got Pete.

RYAN: Scuse me?

JENNY: I do understand it, Ryan. I'm trying to tell you, you can talk to me about it. I know that it's hard for you.

A beat.

RYAN: I need to get on with work.

RYAN goes back to bricklaying.

JENNY: We don't have to talk about it now, but just know, I do get it, and I'm here for you.

LOU: What are you talking about? You just want him to feel like shit.

JENNY: No.

LOU: You want us to feel like shit so we need you.

JENNY: That's not true.

LOU: You thought it'd be the best thing that ever happened, Dad dying. Cos you'd get to be the centre of the world, like a little child. You can't bear that we have our own grief, our own lives, our own ways of coping.

JENNY: How dare you say that to me.

LOU: It's convenient for you to be able to turn him into a saint. And forget that he was a bully as well as the good things, and shit with money along with the good things, and flew off the handle, and tried to control. Now he's not here you can have the perfect husband.

RYAN: All right Lou, that's a bit fucking much, yeah? Shall we calm down a bit?

LOU: I hate this place so much, you know that? If I had my way, a year from now it wouldn't exist. I'd sell it to work, and they'd build on it. They'd tear that house down and put twenty identical new builds over the top, so you couldn't even make out the foundations. And everyone would forget about this life, it would be like it never existed. I'd like to see it buried so deep underground. That's how I'd remember him. That's how I'd remember him, I'd move on.

LOU exits. They watch her go. RYAN walks away from his work.

JENNY: Ryan? Ryan?

SCENE TWO

Early evening. A week later. Night will fall across the course of the scene. JENNY sits on stage in a deck chair round the side of the house, with a big gin and tonic. She has the Bluetooth speakers. Fleetwood Mac's 'The Chain' starts. RYAN enters with his gun. JENNY stops the song.

RYAN: Bit early?

JENNY: After four.

RYAN: Maybe not then. Might have one myself.

JENNY: Don't use my Fever Tree. Why you got that out?

RYAN: Crows. Passes the time.

Enter LOU and PETE from the house, carrying boxes.

RYAN: You packing the car?

LOU: Getting there, yeah.

RYAN: I'm sorry, I would have helped.

LOU: There's still more up there if you want.

RYAN: All right. You wanna come with, Mum?

Silence.

PETE: Guess not then.

RYAN exits towards the house, leaving the gun and bullet box on the bench as he goes. PETE exits towards the car.

LOU: Actually this one's ridiculous.

JENNY: Why?

LOU: School stuff, and – I don't even know. I don't need to take it all with me.

JENNY: Leave it here then.

LOU: Not cos I don't care about it. I just won't need it over there.

JENNY: What's in it, what school?

LOU: Year eleven I think.

JENNY: Let me see?

LOU puts the box down by JENNY. JENNY pokes through it.

JENNY: Oh, look. Oh leave that here with me.

LOU: Why?

JENNY: Let me have a look through all that, that's – I'll put it in the attic later.

LOU: All right. Nearly done now.

JENNY: Yeah?

LOU: Couple more loads and we're done. It'd mean a lot to me if you and Pete could make up a little bit, before we go. I don't want bad feeling. I don't think there has to be any, really.

JENNY: I'll talk to him.

LOU: Will you?

JENNY: I wanted to anyway.

LOU: Thank you.

JENNY: What will you do for your dinner tonight?

LOU: Probably get a Chinese.

JENNY: Lovely.

LOU: What about you?

JENNY: I've got that vegetable soup still left over, I think we'll have that.

LOU: Well I'll see you tomorrow at the airport then. If you wanna come?

JENNY: If you're really going, I'll be there. If you're really going, I'll wave you off.

LOU: OK.

JENNY: Gimme a hug.

They hug.

JENNY: I love you darling.

LOU: Love you too Mum.

Enter PETE.

LOU: I was just saying we'll be off in a minute, won't we.

PETE: Guess we're nearly done, yeah.

LOU: So. I'll get another box I think.

PETE: All right. I'll follow you up in a minute.

LOU: Oh right.

PETE: All good. See you in a minute.

LOU: OK.

LOU exits.

PETE: All right?

JENNY: Hard thing, moving out of a house, isn't it. You leave a lot of things behind you didn't know you weren't going to be able to take with you.

PETE: Yeah. Before we go I thought I should check we were all right?

JENNY: You and me?

PETE: I know it's upsetting, Lou leaving.

JENNY: Yes.

PETE: And I know we haven't really talked since last week. I've felt like you didn't wanna hear from me.

JENNY: That's about right, yeah. But it's fine. You won. That hurts. It's fine.

PETE: Well as long as we're all right going forwards.

JENNY: You've always been good with both my children.

PETE: I feel very lucky I'm marrying Lou.

JENNY: So you should.

PETE: I'm sorry if I've caused a bit of tension between you and Ryan.

JENNY: There's no tension between Ryan and me.

PETE: That's great. I'm only saying, I don't want to be the cause of any aggro. If you ended up chasing him away.

JENNY: I don't think that's about to happen.

PETE: That's great you think that.

JENNY: I'm so lucky to have someone around who knows my kids so well, and can tell me what they're thinking.

PETE: I'm sorry I've offended you.

JENNY: You're going to be part of my family, but I'd be grateful if you left my business to me, all right? I think I have the right to feel what I feel, and speak as I choose to.

PETE: All right.

JENNY: Thank you.

PETE: Once we're gone, though. And things have settled. I do think it'd be worth your while taking some time to think about the way you've behaved this last week.

JENNY: Do you.

PETE: Yeah, I do. And the whole last year, actually Jenny, if I'm honest. I think it'd be good if you thought about who it is you put first. Cos I don't think it's Lou or Ryan very often. And I think they've actually deserved that. I think they've needed that. And haven't got it. Might be good to think about that.

JENNY: I see.

PETE: I'll leave you to it.

PETE turns to leave.

JENNY: And what are you going to do about that?

PETE: What? Oh.

JENNY: Just walking away from it, are you? Not your problem now you're out of here.

PETE: It's working fine.

JENNY: But you'll leave him with the risk of being discovered.

PETE: Ryan's all right. He can keep his head down. What else could I do?

JENNY: Well you could take it apart again.

PETE: It's working fine.

JENNY: Or I could call the police I spose, get them to take it apart. I probably shouldn't, course, you're still on parole, aren't you. So that would actually affect you quite severely.

PETE: What are you doing, Jenny?

JENNY: You're not having my daughter, you little piece of shit. You're not talking to me like that. We let you spend half your childhood here, when you could have been on that shit estate. We cooked you dinner when your mum couldn't be fucked. We gave you more than anyone else has ever given you, you are not going to talk to me like that.

PETE: What are you going to do?

JENNY: If she leaves this farm tonight, I'll call Kev and tell him exactly what you've done. If she sets foot off this farm.

PETE: It's too late, Jenny.

JENNY: You have to tell her. Tell her you've changed your mind.

PETE: I'm not gonna do that.

LOU and RYAN enter, carrying boxes,

LOU: This is the last of it, I reckon. You two all right?

JENNY: Fine.

LOU: You sure you don't mind keeping all that stuff in the loft?

JENNY: Of course not, that's fine.

LOU: Thanks. I guess this is us, then.

JENNY: Unless you had anything you wanted to say, Pete?

PETE: Jenny.

LOU: What's the problem?

PETE: You shouldn't do this.

JENNY: Fuck you.

LOU: Mum!

PETE: Jenny says she's gonna call the police. If I take you away this evening. And tell them about the pipe.

LOU: Fuck's sake.

JENNY: He is not your life, Lou. You're making a mistake.

RYAN: Mum, shut up, please.

JENNY: Ryan.

RYAN: All you're doing is pushing her away. It doesn't even work.

JENNY: She needs to hear it.

RYAN: If you called the police I'd just say I did it.

JENNY: I wouldn't let you. They wouldn't believe you.

RYAN: I bet they would. It wouldn't even work, Mum, stop fucking up.

LOU: I have to go.

JENNY: Lou.

LOU: No, Mum, you've blown this. This was meant to be when we said goodbye, this was meant to be friendly. I can't believe you. Don't come to the airport tomorrow, all right? I don't want to see you.

JENNY: No.

LOU: Ryan, I'll see you tomorrow before we fly.

RYAN: All right.

LOU: I'll be in the car.

PETE: Yeah.

JENNY: Please.

LOU: No, Mum, not now.

LOU exits. JENNY breaks down in tears.

PETE: Hey. Hey, Jenny.

PETE kneels down next to her.

PETE: I'm sorry.

JENNY: Get off me.

PETE stands.

PETE: Gonna miss you mate.

RYAN: Me too. I'm sorry.

PETE: All done now.

RYAN: Remember the first time you ever came round here? Year seven. And your mum was an hour late to pick you back up, and it rained, and you wouldn't wait inside in case she didn't see you. So we stood under that tree and took turns playing *Pokemon Blue*.

PETE: Yeah.

PETE: *(He gestures to the pipe.)* You sure you know what you're doing with that?

RYAN: I'm fine.

PETE: And if anyone does find out –

RYAN: It's fine. No one else needs to have been involved.

PETE: You sure?

RYAN: Be my turn anyway, won't it. To go down for something. I'll be all right. I don't need my hand held, it's all right.

PETE: See you at the airport then.

RYAN: All right.

PETE exits.

RYAN: Mum you are a fucking prize idiot.

JENNY: She didn't really mean I can't come to the airport, do you think?

RYAN: I don't know, Mum. I think she might have done.

JENNY: Maybe you could call her. Call her in a few hours and see if I can come.

RYAN: Maybe.

JENNY: Or in the morning.

RYAN: All right, all right.

RYAN: She was always gonna move back out one day.

JENNY: Never thought it'd be Dubai though. I thought more Basingstoke or Southampton.

RYAN: I think we ought to meet with Lou's firm about that offer they made us.

JENNY: Oh.

RYAN: I think I'd like do that, if that's OK with you.

JENNY: Ryan.

RYAN: The bank want to repossess us, Mum. I know you won't talk about it, I know you'd rather pretend it's not happening, but they want to shut it all down. Maybe it's time to stop hiding away from that, start coming up with a plan.

JENNY: We'll turn the corner.

RYAN: People don't get out of our kind of debt just by grafting. You must know that. Don't you know that? We're in too deep, Dad left us in so deep. Eighty grand on credit cards alone, Mum.

JENNY: So you're pissed your mate left and now it's your father's fault?

RYAN: I didn't say that. How long do you keep doing something that makes you unhappy before it's time to change?

JENNY: Everything we could possibly do would make us unhappy right now. That's how grief happens. Like oil over everything. Drowning everything, all your life you see it through this slick. We have to keep going, that's all. We just have to keep going and believe we'll come out of this feeling.

RYAN: I'm really sorry, but I think I might have stopped believing that. I don't think you can live all your life saying the reason you're unhappy is something that happened last year. When maybe the problem's what's happening now, and you could change it if you only lifted up your head. I never thought about doing anything other than this, always thought this place would be my life. But look at what Lou's doing. It's like she found a trapdoor, and now she's in another world, and she doesn't have to deal with any of this. She can just breathe out.

JENNY: You're overreacting cos your friend's gone away.

RYAN: What?

JENNY: If Pete doesn't like it, neither do you. You were the same about olives.

RYAN: Mum.

JENNY: It's not real, Ryan. What you're feeling, it's natural, everyone thinks they could be doing better. That's what it's like. You went somewhere else, you'd be just as unhappy.

RYAN: Would you want me to keep going if you knew for sure that I didn't want to be here?

JENNY: I never make you do anything. I've never made you do anything all your life. Just don't be stupid, Ryan, don't rush, don't do the wrong thing.

RYAN: I wish you wouldn't call me stupid. Dad used to call me stupid all the time. If he'd told me I was bright, maybe I would have been. I wish we'd sat down the day we got back from the wake and said what we really thought. I thought I was doing what he would have wanted, I wish I could ask him. How can someone be there one day and then just not exist the next? I don't even understand it. I think we've tried very hard not to think about what's happened, haven't we.

JENNY: Yes.

RYAN: And all let each other have our time.

JENNY: Yes.

RYAN: I know I haven't talked. I don't know how to talk about this stuff. But I think that's part of why Lou had to leave, though, don't you? It gets to feel like you can't breathe, doesn't it. Maybe it's time to breathe out, Mum. We can't live as if we think he might come back.

JENNY: I know.

RYAN: We can't keep doing things just for him.

JENNY: You know it will be the end? Of cooked breakfasts and hardback books, and wellingtons and life outdoors, and open fires, and family meals together. No more time with the view all around you. You know that will end.

RYAN: But he died, Mum. And maybe all that went with him.

JENNY: This is our home.

RYAN: No, home was a time when we were together. I'm gonna get a drink. D'you want another?

JENNY: Yeah.

RYAN: Then maybe we can start on dinner.

JENNY: All right.

RYAN: And can I call the developers in the morning?

JENNY: All right.

RYAN exits. A moment. Then…

JENNY: Oh, my love, they're going away from me. And no one sees how much it hurts. I wish you were here to hold us. I didn't know it would finish so fast. What a terrible thing it is to marry someone. And tell someone I will give all of my love to you, and you can have all of my spare time, I will plant the roots of my life in you, **all in the sure and certain knowledge it will one day end.** I did the wrong thing coming here. I shouldn't have let you bring me here, so stupid. You're not even hearing me now, are you. You're not listening to me, you're not listening!

JENNY walks over and picks up the rifle. She holds it up to the light. Then she takes aim and shoots the pipe. The pipe breaks. Oil starts rushing out of it, drenching JENNY. Enter RYAN, carrying wine.

RYAN: Mum.

RYAN puts down the wine and the glasses he's carrying, and rushes to her, trying to get hold of her.

JENNY shoots the pipe again.

RYAN: Mum, what are you doing?

RYAN has his arms around his mother. He has stopped her attacking the pipe. He gets the rifle out of her hands and chucks it away from her, and pulls her away from the pipe, which is raining oil onto the ground. JENNY cries, and collapses to the floor.

JENNY: I wish I could burn it away. I wanna give it chemo till it's all burned away.

RYAN: What the fuck have you done?

JENNY: Get them back. He needs to fix it, get them back. Call Pete and tell him to turn the car around.

RYAN: No, Mum, I'm not gonna do that. They've got out, I won't make them come back.

JENNY: Just call him.

RYAN: I won't.

JENNY: But look at it, we can't leave it like that.

RYAN: I know.

JENNY: So what are we going to do? Can you close that up?

RYAN: I don't know.

RYAN realises.

JENNY: Ryan?

RYAN: I'm gonna call the maintenance line.

JENNY: No.

RYAN: That's what we have to do. Is the number inside?

JENNY: They'll know what's been happening. They'll know what we've done.

RYAN: Yeah but that's what has to happen, Mum. Lou and Pete have gone now. And it's my turn.

JENNY: Please.

RYAN: It is, it's my turn.

JENNY: You can't.

RYAN: I think I want to. I've felt so fucking bad for so long. Maybe if I do something right, that'll help me.

JENNY: I'd be on my own.

RYAN: There's nothing to be done. They've gone now, they're free of it. Let's give them that. I'd better go in and find the number.

JENNY: Please.

RYAN: What would Dad have wanted?

JENNY: I don't fucking know. I'm so angry at him. How dare he go and die? I can't hear him any more.

RYAN: I know. Look at that, up there. That's the only star I know besides Orion. When I get scared I tell myself it might be Dad. And he's looking out for me. Pointing the way.

JENNY: Why that one?

RYAN: Cos that's the pole star. First star in the evening. That's how you know where north is.

END.

WWW.OBERONBOOKS.COM

Follow us on www.twitter.com/@oberonbooks
& www.facebook.com/OberonBooksLondon

www.ingramcontent.com/pod-product-compliance
Ingram Content Group UK Ltd.
Pitfield, Milton Keynes, MK11 3LW, UK
UKHW020720280225
455688UK00012B/441